KIDNAPPED

The untold story of
my abduction

Chloe Ayling
KIDNAPPED

JOHN BLAKE

Published by John Blake Publishing,
2.25, The Plaza,
535 Kings Road,
Chelsea Harbour
London, SW10 0SZ

www.johnblakebooks.com

www.facebook.com/johnblakebooks 🅕
twitter.com/jblakebooks 🅔

This edition published in 2018

ISBN: 978-1-78606-884-2

British Library Cataloguing-in-Publication Data:

A catalogue record for this book is available from the British Library.

Design by www.envydesign.co.uk

Printed and bound in Great Britain by Clays Ltd, Elcograf S.p.A.

1 3 5 7 9 10 8 6 4 2

Papers used by John Blake Publishing are natural, recyclable products made from wood grown in sustainable forests. The manufacturing processes conform to the environmental regulations of the country of origin.

Every attempt has been made to contact the relevant copyright-holders, but some were unobtainable. We would be grateful if the appropriate people could contact us.

John Blake Publishing is an imprint of Bonnier Publishing
www.bonnierpublishing.com

Contents

Foreword

Dear reader,

My name is Chloe Ayling. I am the victim of a kidnapping plot that has made headlines around the world. I have survived an ordeal that is the stuff of nightmares and something I will live with for the rest of my life. What happened to me has been broken down and analysed by the police, investigators, international media, and by everyone and anyone who thinks they might know the truth. But what I am about to tell you now, every single word printed in this book, is the truth. So if you want to know exactly what happened to me, carry on reading.

If you still think this is a fictitious story that I have made up because I'm an attention seeker I suggest you read something else. I don't have time for you or your scepticism. Going through what I have gone through has taught me one thing: you never know what is going to happen; you never know what is round the corner. You have to live every moment.

I am a mother. My son is too young yet to understand what has happened to me but one day he will and I will show him this book. You have to understand as well that I am not prepared to talk about him in this book. This is *my* story – of course he is part of my world, but I don't want to be involving him in this horror. I want to protect him from it. Does that make me sound cold? My mum says I'm cold. She says I don't get it from her. She brought me up by herself, as a single mum, and so blames my dad for my cold nature. I must have got it from him, she says. Why else would a father not see his daughter? I must be cold like him. Cold, unemotional, distant…whatever you think, I won't be guilty of overexposing my son.

I am guilty of one thing, though. Previously I told of my experience in a very black-and-white manner because it has helped me cope with it. That was my strategy, to be matter-of-fact because it helped me distance myself from the hell I endured. But not anymore. Now I am ready to face everything and expose every little detail for the first time. Do I seem tough? I'm not. I have spent days crying and crying over what happened, being in fear for my life, made to believe I would be sold as a sex slave. I have been manipulated, drugged, targeted, and now character-assassinated as a liar and attention seeker.

I am only human. I want to put this behind me, to move on with my life, to forge a new path for myself free from the horrors I have experienced. I am not a warrior or a charity campaigner, but I am a person who is willing to help others who have been in my situation. I refuse to be labelled as Chloe Ayling the kidnapped model any more. I refuse to be labelled a victim for ever.

I am a survivor and this is my story…

Chloe Ayling

CHAPTER 1

It started with Paris...

'I was happy to be wandering around a city I didn't know. I was relaxed... I was fearless.'

There are some moments in my life I will never forget – moments ingrained in my head for ever. I don't think they will ever let me neglect them. Like the moment I saw a man in a black ski mask force a syringe into my skin...

I also remember, as clear as day, where I was when my agent, Phil, rang me about a modelling assignment. It was a modelling assignment that would change my life for ever.

'Go, Nylah, go on!' I unhooked the lead from my excitable beagle and let her scamper off across the fields. That freedom to run, that joy of being able to gallop at speed in search of a scent – it wasn't a chore taking my dog for a walk at all; we'd often head out for an hour, an hour and a half. It was wonderful. My phone started ringing as I watched her.

The problem with having a dog who liked to track was that sometimes she was so engrossed in a smell that she didn't come back when she should. I answered my phone to Phil as I headed over in Nylah's direction, trying to keep an eye on her.

I signed with Phil and the Supermodel Agency in 2016. I always wanted to be a model. I knew I was too short for fashion modelling – you have to be 5ft 8ins – but I could do commercial and glamour. That was OK with me – I knew I would be able to get enough jobs in that side of the industry. I would never be Kate Moss, but if I worked hard and did lots of modelling assignments I could make a good living out of it.

I suppose the thought of travelling around the world was also a big incentive. I loved the idea of visiting different countries; that was so exciting. I didn't mind being on my own – I like my own company and I can look after myself on trips like these. I didn't have a worry in the world about visiting new places. Besides, the opportunities they give me help me provide for my son. I am a single mum and that is my purpose: to provide for Ashton.

'I have a great job lined up for you, Chloe,' Phil began. 'In Paris. You have been specifically requested by the photographer.'

Right then, right there, were two pitches that Phil knew I wouldn't be able to refuse. Paris! I had never been to Paris before and I was eager to go to new places and do some exploring, be a typical tourist… it was such a perk of the job. I loved doing international jobs; it was a dream to be able to see the world through work. And requested personally? That meant I had made a big impression – they wanted me.

He explained that the shoot was for a new brand of motorbike leathers and the photos would be used in motorbike magazines and on posters around Paris. He said he needed my measurements, which was a bit of a pain. I had given them to him when I joined the agency, but he explained that the leathers would need to be custom-made to fit, and so my measurements needed to be completely accurate. I agreed to go and see him at some point. He always measures the girls himself and I did put it off for a while but, as it was requested by the client in this case, I had no choice.

Besides, the thought of Paris was exciting. Phil emailed me the details of the assignment a little while later and I was disappointed to find that my time in the French capital only stretched to one night. Even my mum said it was a shame when I showed her the email. She liked the thought of me seeing the world and being paid for it. Not that she didn't worry about me. She's a big worrier, my mum, but show me a mum who doesn't worry! It's just who she is, so I do all I can to make sure she has nothing to worry about, texting her three or four times a day when I'm away for shoots, and we always try and speak before bedtime too.

Ashton is looked after whenever I'm away. I always feel a dull ache when I say goodbye. Ashton is my world and I want to protect him, but I know you will read this and maybe feel that I'm neglecting talking about him as much as I could. I am a mother – how can I not talk about my son? I will tell you this about him, and then I want you to understand that for me to cope with what I have been through I have had to compartmentalise him and focus on surviving for his sake. An emotional, hapless wreck I am not and will never be.

I fell pregnant at seventeen years old and I gave birth to him when I was eighteen. I was totally shocked when I found out I was pregnant; it wasn't planned at all. Being completely honest, I was unsure if I wanted to keep him. It was all such a shock, and I was so young, that I didn't think I would cope with a baby. It was just me, Mum and Nylah at home – could we have a baby in the house too? I was still at college and I was worried about how I would be able to study. I was studying Sports Science and really enjoying it. I didn't know how I would manage to keep going, but the head of the college was very understanding. She told me it had happened before, that they would give me time off, and then I could continue my studies once I had settled into motherhood.

No one tells you how painful giving birth is. It was a 24-hour induced labour and was so tiring. I just remember feeling exhausted when Ashton was born. I didn't hold him straight away because I had a forceps delivery and I had to be stitched. It was surreal holding him for the first time but I was so drained I didn't take it in at first. But then, stroking his cheek, nestling against his sweet-smelling head, he was mine and I was his and that is how it will be for ever. We didn't need anyone else, we had each other. So please forgive me if I don't go into any more about him than that. I am his protector. I vowed to be that the first moment I met him.

★ ★ ★

The client had sent Phil the money to book my flights and he asked me which flight times I wanted. My answer was always the same in a situation like this – the earliest one, so I could fit as much sightseeing as possible into the day. I would have the whole day before the photo shoot to see as much of Paris as I could. I might not have long there but I wanted to make the most of it, even if it meant getting up at the crack of dawn to catch the flight.

Phil forwarded me the details of the email, sent from a man called Andre Lazio, the photographer for the shoot. The email is below. Can you see the level of detail included, the directions, the instructions, the way everything is thought of? This wasn't a suspicious email; there wasn't anything to suggest this was a hoax, a plot, or anything untoward. The English wasn't brilliant but there wasn't anything that didn't make sense, or that I didn't understand. Take a look.

From: Andre Lazio [mailto:andre@★★★★★★★★★★.fr]
Sent: Friday, April 7, 2017 3:56 PM
To: Supermodel Agency
Subject: RE: Model booking Paris

Hi Phil,
I have organised a private transfer for Chloe from CDG
Terminal 3 Airport, the driver will be holding a sign with

her name at the arrivals around 12:00 local time. He will take Chloe directly to the Hotel Madeleine Plaza, she will have breakfast included next morning as well as a view for the Madeleine Church, one of the Paris landmarks. Hotel is in Paris centre so the transfer might take anything between 30–45 minutes, dependent on traffic.

She will have to present Passport upon arrival, but they will also require a credit card for a deposit which is very usual for all Paris hotels which obviously will not be charged when everything is in order which I am sure it will. It turns out that Hotel doesn't have a spa access anymore as Booking.com promised, they are happy to refer guests to local spa, and should Chloe wish to use it I am happy to refund for local food expenses up to 150EUR which in total would give Chloe 300EUR expenditure in Paris as it's all still within my budget. I would still advise not to wander too far too late.

She will be picked up at the hotel at 9:00 local time on Friday morning and taken to the studio. All transfers are fully paid for. Upon arrival I will do my best to greet her at the entrance, but should I be inside she can just help herself inside, it doesn't look as nice as previous studio did as we only just moved in, but we needed extra space to expand to film studio as well. Motorbike has been fitted to the floor so there is no chance it could fall during the shoot. Offices are right inside the studio, there are signs all around it as well.

After the photoshoot I will take Chloe to the CDG airport myself to make sure she find right terminal in time

for her returning flight. Please make sure she has return
flight details printed with her as using CDG public wifi
may not prove to be the best option.

Please give her my local mobile number in case
something won't work as it should, but I doubt that will
be the case. 0033 0753 *** ***

Andre

I arrived in Paris on Thursday 20 April and the taxi had
been arranged to pick me up at the airport. I spotted 'Chloe
Ayling' in big black letters being held by the taxi driver as I
went through the arrivals gate.

It was around lunchtime, so I still had a good part of the
day for exploring. I knew exactly where I wanted to go first –
the Eiffel Tower. OK, that is probably pretty typical but that
is where I wanted to go. The taxi took me, as promised on
the email, to the Hotel Madeleine Plaza, which was situated
right in the centre of the capital. It was a beautiful day, so
I decided, after checking in (again, no problem), dumping
my bags in my room and having a quick freshen-up, to head
right out and find that tower. The hotel was surrounded by
gorgeous designer shops and pretty boutiques but I didn't
stop to shop. I had no idea where I was going but I knew if
I kept walking I would find my way eventually. Does that
sound crazy? I was so carefree back then. I didn't worry that
I didn't know exactly where I was going; I was happy to be
wandering around a city I didn't know. I was relaxed, I was
easy-going, I was fearless. I had no idea of any danger.

I walked down a couple of streets before I saw, in the

distance, the tip of the Eifel Tower. So I just kept walking towards it. It was such a long way, but I did it. It was pretty impressive when I got there, so I took a photo and started to walk back to the hotel. It felt even longer on the way back – had I really walked this far?! I was pleased with myself that I remembered the way, though, and I wasn't worried about getting lost or panicking. I didn't have that thought process back then. Nothing scared me. And that night I did something I had always done: I went out for dinner by myself. I didn't think anything of it; it doesn't bother me. I like my own company and I like to experience what I can in a different place. Eating alone might seem strange to some people but I enjoyed it, it wasn't a problem. I went to a restaurant that was about a three-minute walk round the corner from the hotel, as I had walked far enough that day.

I can look back at this sort of thing now, the carefree way it didn't even occur to me that this could be dangerous. Was I naïve? I just didn't worry about anything back then. Now is different. Now I won't go out for dinner or go anywhere by myself. I have changed in the way I respond to people too. I won't talk to anyone or join in their conversations if I don't know them. I don't care if that makes me seem cold or unfriendly – that is my way of protecting myself now. My way of dealing with what has happened. Even writing this, the way things used to be, the things I did… it seems strange. That was a Chloe before all this happened. The Chloe afterwards is different.

It was probably around 11pm when I went back to the hotel room. I hadn't been back long when I started hearing police sirens. Suddenly the night was filled with the noise of the emergency services – a constant wailing going on and on as they sped down the streets. I had no idea what was occurring but something major must have happened. I called my mum. She didn't know what was happening either but she didn't take the news well. 'That's not a good sign,' she said. Then my friend sent me a message: it was a photo message and a screenshot of the news with the words: 'Terror hits Paris as policeman shot on the Champs-Élysées'.

I didn't know what to think. Was I in danger? Were there more terrorists? Had they caught the gunman? I rang Mum again, and then Phil, and they both told me to stay in the hotel. To stay in my room and not go out. My mum needed a lot of reassurance. I told her I wasn't going anywhere until the morning, and even then the taxi had been arranged for me. I wasn't going to be wandering off anywhere. I wasn't worried, I told her. I was fine and I will be fine. I guess I was just too chilled. Nothing really fazed me then. And I couldn't do anything, could I? OK, it was pretty scary but I didn't think I was in any danger.

I went to sleep fairly early that night as I had an early start and didn't really think much of it the next morning when I went down to breakfast. I was sitting in the restaurant having something to eat when the hotel receptionist came over with the telephone and said I had a call. A man's voice came on the line. He introduced himself as Andre, the photographer. He told me that the studio had been burgled overnight. He said everything had been taken – all his camera equipment and lighting gear – and only the motorbike was left. He told me he wasn't able to go ahead with the shoot. He was very apologetic about it but what could he say? You can't take photos without a camera! He told me to get into the taxi that had been arranged to take me to the studio and use it to take me to the airport instead. It was simple enough. OK, it was disappointing not to have done the shoot, but I had been paid in advance and I hadn't lost any money.

I checked out of the hotel and followed the instructions, taking what I thought was the taxi ordered for me to return to the airport. But it wasn't the right taxi; the reference number was different and, when we arrived at the airport, the taxi driver wanted money. He kept signalling that I owed him money when I thought I was in the prepaid taxi. I tried ringing Phil but I knew it wouldn't be any good. He doesn't wake up early and he doesn't answer his phone before 10:30am. That was an annoyance I'd had with him before when I'd had morning jobs. So I found the email containing the shoot details and called the number at the bottom.

I was expecting to speak to Andre again but another man answered and said he would let Andre know. I passed the phone to the taxi driver so he could communicate and understand what was happening. The taxi driver didn't speak any English, so I wasn't able to explain that I was trying to get to the bottom of the mix-up – he didn't understand anything I was saying. I had to use Google Translate in the end to make him understand.

I sometimes think back to this situation. I was annoyed and felt unlucky that I was unable to do a shoot because of the terrorist attack. It was so annoying to me at the time but now I know how lucky I was. The absolute best scenario really…imagine that, imagine being pleased that a terrorist attack had saved me from being kidnapped then.

I had no money on me, as I was due expenses from the shoot, so I hadn't bothered getting any. I sat in the back of the taxi for about forty-five minutes and then a man suddenly appeared at the car window. I got out of the car. This must be Andre, I thought. He had come to sort out the mess. He paid the taxi driver and apologised. It was Andre; he had come to the airport as soon as he got the message, he said.

He looked young for a photographer but then, the photographers I've met all look different; there isn't a stereotypical look. He had sunglasses on and he kept them on as we talked. He was very apologetic and seemed really sad about the burglary and that the photo shoot didn't happen. He kept saying that at least the motorbike was still there; they took everything else but he still had the bike.

'I can't believe what happened last night,' I said to him. 'It was so scary.' But he didn't respond. He changed the subject, telling me how fed up he was with Paris, that this burglary was the last straw and he was going back to Milan, where he used to live. 'Paris isn't safe any more. It's not how it used to be,' he said.

The whole conversation lasted for a few minutes and I genuinely felt sorry for him. He told me that when the insurance money came through, and he'd bought new equipment, that he would rearrange the shoot. Saying he didn't like Paris any more sowed the seed that the location might be somewhere different. He gave me expenses for the day, as I would now have to wait in the airport until my flight, which wasn't due until much later. And then he was gone.

I texted Mum to let her know I was at the airport and then I just waited. I pretty much sat on my phone all day. I can lose myself for hours on social media. So I just sat there, on my phone, waiting. There was lots of extra security at the airport, and then my flight got delayed, but I made it home eventually. It wasn't a completely wasted trip, I thought to myself. I had seen the Eiffel Tower and, by the sounds of it, I would be rebooked and maybe go to somewhere like Milan next; that would be cool.

That was how my mind worked then. Not a care in the world. Nothing fazed me.

★ ★ ★

'Dubai here we come!' My friend Danielle and I were toasting our excitement as we sat in Heathrow Airport having dinner. It was early May, and Paris was now a distant memory as I was about to jet off on another job, this time with my best friend Danielle Sellers. Working with Danielle on modelling assignments is great fun – it doesn't really feel like work.

The job we had booked in Dubai was meant to be for music videos and YouTube videos and the client had asked for us both specifically. My phone rang as we sat eating and chatting and I looked down at the caller ID. It was Phil.

Danielle doesn't like Phil. She was with a different management agency. She had tried to convince me to leave him and find another agency. I dismissed her concerns. I was fine where I was, I told her. Besides, Phil had just told me that Andre had emailed him and wanted to reschedule the Paris shoot – only this time it was going to be in Milan. I had never been to Milan and I was very excited. I had a big grin on my face when Phil told me. It was scheduled for the beginning of July, which seemed like ages away, but I remember being really happy.

I didn't even mind when the Dubai job fell through. We had just flown out there when we heard there was a massive cock-up over the booking or something. But, instead of catching a flight straight home, Danielle and I were invited to stay anyway and have a mini-holiday with the client. It was amazing: the beaches, the nightclubs, the food…we were out there for five days and it was incredible. And I had my best friend with me to enjoy it too! In the end it was a cool, girly holiday.

On 14 June I celebrated my twentieth birthday with Danielle and we went out for dinner. Well, we actually went out on the following evening, as I spent my birthday doing a photo shoot for the *Daily Star*. It was on location at a beach and I really didn't want to be working on my birthday! I was too tired to go out that night, so Danielle arranged everything for the following evening. We went to Drama in Park Lane – a somewhat high-end nightclub. She had planned the whole evening for me and I had no idea what was happening but it was a great night.

I joined Phil and his agency in August 2016, and I was offered Page 3 in September that year. I knew when I started I wouldn't be paid; it was more about building my profile and increasing my social media interest. This led to YouTube videos and my social media profile quickly rose. I was getting booked for jobs quite regularly. Working for *Sixty6* magazine helped a lot too. I would only go to clubs for events, as I'm not a big drinker and being in a nightclub when you're not drinking is quite hard! If I'm totally honest, and I know this won't sound very cool, I only go out very rarely, on special occasions like my birthday. I don't even like clubbing. I prefer to be at home in the evenings. I like being home and chilling with the dog, knowing my son is sleeping soundly upstairs and I can go and tuck him up, stroke his hair or just watch him peacefully lying there.

On Friday 30 June I received the email from Phil about the rescheduled photo shoot, now taking place in Milan. I read it through and remember thinking it was very thorough. There wasn't anything in that email that suggested anything other than a fairly standard modelling assignment.

From: Supermodel Agency
Date: Fri, 30 Jun 2017 at 11:09
Subject: Milan
To: Chloe
  FORWARDED EMAIL
  Chloe is staying at Best Western Plus Hotel Galles [★★★★] (Piazza Lima, 2, 20124 Milano). Very well-known hotel and my uncle works there. I have managed to get Chloe fantastic deal, there's a lot of extras involved that I can't even name, including free spa, gym,

swimming pool etc. Best to ask hotel staff to see what has been included, of course breakfast is included as well.

Milano taxis have set charges from airports to the city centre and vice versa so if Chloe could take few extra euros just in case and I will refund her here, no problem at all. After the shoot I will drive her to Malpensa myself as we will finish approximately 3pm. Can you please ask her to book a taxi for approximately 8.15am to make sure she arrives at the studio for 9am.

Studio address is Via Carlo Bianconi 7, 20139 Milano. I have attached a small picture for reference, but it's only a small street so I am sure she can find it easily. I live just opposite of the studio. We are still preparing everything and I am afraid motorbike cannot be screwed to the floor this time, we will secure it with the straps instead and photoshop it afterwards. The whole shot is on the green screen as well.

I will do my best to greet Chloe at the door but if not we will leave it opened as the studio is on the back of the building, front will be converted into film studio so she can just walk straight in, there is a sign on the door that it's Belissmafique. I am sure you know the business so there's always some final arrangements to do and I might be on the back of the building. On the 10th I have a man coming to fix AirCon, right now with heatwaves he is the busiest man in Milano, but I will make sure it's working fine when Chloe is here.

My private phone number is 35 **** ****, so if there's anything to discuss please let me know. I am sure

everything will be fine in my home city and I am looking
forward to see Chloe in lot better circumstances than last
time!
   Andre

So there you have it. The details of the job that would seal
my fate. I read through the email and then put the phone
down and thought nothing else of it. I was so excited to be
going to Milan; it was like a dream come true. A dream that
turned into a nightmare.

CHAPTER 2

Milan

'I tried to open my mouth but I couldn't.
There was tape across it.'

MONDAY 10 JULY

The alarm clock's shrill tone rang out, invading the stillness of the house. It was 4am but I didn't need waking up. I'd hardly slept. I'd probably dozed for about an hour but was wide awake by 3am. It's always the way when I have an early start for a modelling assignment – I am worried about missing the alarm, and then missing the taxi and then missing my flight. It was the morning of my flight to Milan and I went into Mum's room to say goodbye. She reminded me to keep in contact and I promised I would. I promised her I would text her when I arrived.

Nylah wagged her tail at me as I left the house and slipped

into the taxi waiting outside. It was a dark, chilly morning and it didn't take us long to get to Gatwick Airport as there wasn't much traffic on the roads. I was excited about going to Milan but, if I'm honest, I was more excited about what I would be doing on Wednesday – flying to Ibiza! I was going with my photographer, Danny. We would get some photos for my portfolio and have some fun too. It was work but it probably wouldn't feel too much like hard work. I just had to get the Milan job done and then I would fly home the next evening and then fly out to the party island early the following morning. OK, so I might be a bit tired but I was going to Ibiza!

I landed in Milan around 10am and, instead of doing my usual touristy thing of trying to see the sights, I decided I should perhaps have a nap. I took a taxi straight to the hotel and decided I definitely needed to catch up on some sleep. I called Mum and Phil to let them know I had arrived, and then I checked into the Best Western Plus Hotel Galles and went straight up to my room for a shower and a quick nap. Well, I say it was a nap, that was the plan, but I didn't actually wake up until 7pm. My sightseeing plans were definitely out of the window then, but the area around the hotel was still lively, so I decided to head out and investigate. And I was pretty hungry by that point too, so I ventured out onto the main street, Corso Buenos Aires. There were a lot of clothes shops still open and I ventured into a couple and ended up buying myself some new bikinis for Ibiza. I was definitely ready to go now. Not long, I thought to myself, as I started looking for a restaurant to have a quick dinner.

I found a small place and it wasn't long before a couple of men tried to talk to me. You know what? I didn't care. Then it wasn't an issue. It was just one of those things. My problem is I'm too nice. I always reply to their questions when they try to start conversations with me – really I should tell them to go away but that doesn't seem very polite. And because I don't tell them to go away they then think I want to talk some more, and they end up following me down the street. These guys, they are always in their thirties and invariably harmless and it happened all the time, so I guess I was just used to it. I would laugh it off. No harm done. I was naïve; I didn't think anything of it. If they were really persistent and wanted to talk for a long time, then I would tell them I had a boyfriend and they would usually take that as an answer.

After dinner I went back to the hotel and used the gym for a bit. I went on the treadmill and then decided, as it was nearly midnight and I had an early start tomorrow, that I'd better head back to my room to get some sleep. I messaged my mum before I went to sleep, as I always do, and then set the alarm for 7am.

TUESDAY 11 JULY

I hit the snooze button one last time…it was 7.10am, too early to get up. One last snooze wouldn't hurt. I would snooze all day if I could. Eventually, at 7.20am, I got up and got ready, had a quick shower and got dressed. I was wearing a pink velvet bodysuit, blue jeans with white markings, white Adidas trainers, a jacket and a cap. I tied my hair back and put on some make-up. I always wear make-up, which, yes, is pretty pointless 'cos you have to take it all off again and have it reapplied for the photo shoot, but I don't care. I can't arrive and meet people I have never met before with no make-up.

I went down for breakfast and then came back up to my room and grabbed my suitcase. Do I get excited about photo shoots? Not really, it was a normal routine for me. Besides, this time the following day I would be on my way to Ibiza, and how exciting would that be? So yes, I guess I was probably a little bit more excited than usual that morning, as I was thinking about Ibiza, but this photo shoot was just routine stuff, it was just work, and I wanted to get it done.

I ordered a taxi from Reception and checked out about 8.15/8.30am. The taxi arrived and I hopped in. I gave the driver the address I had from the email and we were off. I had twenty minutes to look at the passing scenery as we drove through the city in the morning traffic.

We pulled up outside a building. 'Number seven,' the driver said, and pointed to a large building. The address was Via Carlo Bianconi 7, 20139, Milano. Both the taxi driver and I could see the number 7 so we both assumed this was the correct address. I thanked him, paid him and got out.

I pulled my suitcase behind me as I tried the handle to let myself in but it was locked. There was no way I could get in. I looked at my phone and found the email with the instructions. I was definitely here at the right time, and it said that the door would be open and for me to come through… It was a bit strange that the place looked deserted but I thought perhaps there was another entrance.

I decided to call the number at the bottom of the email: 'Andre's private number', it said. It had worked when I'd called him in Paris – when he came to my rescue in that taxi – so I was sure he could explain where I needed to go now.

I heard the dialling tone and then ringing as I waited for Andre to answer. A man whose voice I didn't recognise answered.

'Hi, who's this?' I asked. It didn't sound like Andre.

'Daniel,' said the voice.

'Where is Andre?' I said. 'I am here for his photo shoot.'

'Andre doesn't get here until nine but I'm in the studio, so just come in,' came the reply.

'I can't, the door is locked,' I said.

'No it's not. I am here,' said Daniel.

'OK, I must have been trying the wrong door. Where do I need to go?' I looked around, but there wasn't another obvious door that I could see.

He explained where I had to go. He stayed on the phone as he directed me down the street. There was an opening in the street and a gateway with garages and then I saw a smaller building, which had gold frames on the door, a lot like the first bigger building I had tried. It seemed similar. It must be part of the bigger building, I thought, part of the same complex. As I was on the phone to him while I was walking along, I knew it was the right place. 'I'm here,' I said, and I hung up.

What did I think when I saw the outside of that building? The honest truth was absolutely nothing. I can't tell you how many modelling assignments are in disused warehouses or old buildings or strange-looking studios. As soon as you go inside there is noise, there is camera equipment everywhere and they are set up in their own little world. I suppose the silence that hit me when I entered the building was, looking back now, a clue that all wasn't quite right. It was dead silent. Studios are never quiet. There is always music playing from somewhere. I held my mobile in one hand and my suitcase in the other and I entered.

I opened the door. I was expecting to see Daniel but there was no one. I put my luggage down in front of me and held my purse and phone in the other hand.

I could see black, seven-foot-high wooden boards right in front of me. They weren't ceiling height but they were tall enough to make a specific path in the warehouse building. I followed it round to the right and it took me to a corridor. There was a door slightly open at the end of the corridor and another, also slightly open, to my left. The one to my left had the word 'studio' on it, in big, black, capital letters. It was still eerily silent. I didn't quite know what to do so I put my hand on the door handle – and that is when it happened. Before I had a chance to open it. Did I actually touch the handle? Did I feel the handle or did I just reach out, ready to touch it, to open it? Things like this I can't remember because what occurred next happened so quickly.

A man came at me from behind. I felt a gloved hand on my mouth and over my nose and I panicked. I couldn't breathe. I just wanted to move his thumb from my nose so I could breathe. My head was being held back so tightly, so strongly, and I felt another arm pin me, across my neck, back against my attacker. Then I saw another man, a masked man, rush in in front of me. A ski mask, a black ski mask with two eyeholes and a mouth-hole, and I saw a needle… God no! What was happening? I tried to wriggle, to move, to fight, but I couldn't. I was holding onto my purse and phone so tightly. My first thought was, Am I being robbed?

My right arm…he had grabbed my right arm and my sleeve was being pushed up. The man behind me was holding me so tightly, one arm round my neck and the other across my face, over my mouth and nose, trying to keep me from screaming out. I tried so hard to move, flinging myself about as much as I could, but his grip didn't loosen at all.

I was wrestled to the floor. I was no match for the two of them. The masked man was over me, the syringe was now going in, piercing my skin.

I can only describe that feeling as an odd mixture of fright and calm. I had been fighting back the whole time until then but I had to give in. There was nothing I could do. When I was younger I had a problem with one of my teeth and I remember being sedated. It was like that. It is a strange feeling of knowing you are losing control. Only this time I was there one minute and then I was gone. It wasn't like I had time to prepare for that feeling, I didn't get that drowsy sensation; I was just completely wiped out. As soon as the syringe was in me I was gone. A heavy black wave of darkness descended over me. That was it. Everything went black.

★ ★ ★

The jolt stirs me and I groggily try to open my eyes. I am trying to wake up. Am I dreaming? What is happening? I don't know what's going on. I am half aware of movement... I am being jolted again...

Was I in a plane, a boat? I had no clue. It was noisy, my brain was groggy. It was pitch black. I could hear noises but I was too drowsy to work out what was going on. I forced myself to try to stay awake. Suddenly my mind clicked in and I realised something was wrong with my face. It felt different, tight. I could feel something on my mouth but my brain wasn't quite registering what it was at that point. I knew something didn't feel right but my hands and my brain weren't quite coordinating. The drugs I had been given were still in effect and I couldn't work out where I was, what was happening. I felt dopey. Every movement was an effort.

I tried to open my mouth but I couldn't – there was tape across it. I moved my hands up and tried to peel it off. It took me ages. Or what felt like ages. I was trying to tell my brain to tell my hands to move to my face and eventually I managed to peel it off. At last I could breathe. I needed to breathe, I needed to focus. I closed my eyes and took in several deep breaths but all I could manage were shallow, hot intakes of air. I was trying to register what was going on. I was lying on my side and I could feel metal round my wrists. Handcuffs. I could feel them around my ankles too. There was a black, rubbery material all around me. I could feel it on top of me, underneath me, everywhere… I was in a bag. Oh my God, I was in a bag and I was in handcuffs!

I cannot describe the feeling that went through me then because, in all honesty, there is no feeling I could associate with it. I didn't process, at that point, what it all meant. I couldn't; it was too much to understand. My mind was focusing on a small hole in front of me – a gap in the bag. I became all-consumed with trying to get my hands through that gap. Fixated with it. It was right in front of my face and I tried to move my arms up and put them through the hole, to make the hole bigger. Everything felt like a huge effort because I still felt groggy, but I was desperate to make this hole bigger, to get more light, to get more air. The hole was my lifeline through which I could breathe.

It was probably only a matter of minutes but I wasn't thinking of anything else at that point. I couldn't get my hands free of the handcuffs but I was sure if I kept trying I could get my arms through the hole. I'm not sure why I thought I needed to do this but it was my focus. Make the hole bigger, make the hole bigger…

That's it! I had done it. I managed to get them through. Or maybe I had moved the zip…but suddenly the hole was bigger. Suddenly it was lighter. I think I had dislodged the zip somehow. I don't think I managed to rip the bag but the zip had loosened and suddenly there was more light. In the blink of an eye there was more light.

But the light showed me clearly where I was, and there

was no escape from the realisation I was now facing. I was in the boot of a car, and we were moving. And I was in a bag and handcuffed. In a weird sense of calm, I knew what I had to do. I needed to stop the car; I needed to get the driver's attention and stop the car. I tried to bang and knock this thing above me, the parcel shelf. That was my next goal… I remember all I wanted to do was to get the driver's attention. I called out: 'Driver! Driver!'

I thought that maybe the person driving had no idea what he was transporting. Maybe the driver had nothing to do with the two masked men. Maybe he would save me if I got his attention. There were a lot of maybes but right then I didn't have anything else. Both hands were out now. I felt a screw, or the cap of something… I started twisting and unscrewing it. I was trying anything. I was frantic. I felt the cap or screw come right off and all of a sudden there was water. My hand was swimming in water. I could hear the engine rumbling, the car noises, the radio… If I could just get the driver's attention he would realise there was a person in the car and he would help me. I kept trying to bang the parcel shelf, to knock it off. I used the flats of both my palms to bang it above my head. Any noise I could make I did.

'Driver! Driver!' I tried to shout but I was still feeling drugged, so I ended up just speaking loudly. Everything still seemed a major effort. I had no energy. I was using all my energy to hit the parcel shelf.

Bang, bang, bang – then it was off. It fell on top of me and suddenly there was more daylight coming in.

Then the car came to a sudden stop. My plan had worked.

We had jerked to a stop and I was jolted in the boot but we had stopped. I waited. I looked through the gap and I could make out a face…a hairy face. It was the smallest glimpse but I could see a beard. He must have seen me look at him. He glanced down and I'm sure he saw me peer through and see him through the hole. It's funny what noises you hear – the creak of a handbrake coming up seemed so loud. The doors clicking open. And then the boot was opening. I was facing the wrong way, towards the inside of the car, not the opening of the boot, so I twisted my neck round to see what was going to happen. Two masked men stood before me, peering at me. I just wanted to talk, for them to hear me. I wanted to know what was going on.

'Where are we? What's happening?' The words tumbled out and it was such an effort to talk but I wanted to know what was going on. I asked again, 'Where am I?' What's happening?' I just wanted to know a reason. I wanted to know why I had been taken. But they just stood there in complete silence. Nothing.

I probably sounded incoherent, but I didn't care. It might seem strange but up until that point my brain hadn't fully registered what I was wearing. I was still in my pink velvet bodysuit and socks but everything else had gone. My cap, jacket, jeans and trainers. My hair was down too. I had arrived at the studio with it up but now it was all over the place, matted and sweaty. I could feel my hairband somewhere still in it, tangled and stuck. I never wear my hair down if it's hot outside of a photo shoot. Why had they taken it down? They still didn't say a word as I lay there, suddenly feeling very exposed. One of them leant in and put the tape back over my mouth. They tightened the handcuffs around my wrists. Then they moved the parcel shelf back over me and zipped up the bag again. It was all in complete silence. The boot slammed shut and then I felt the car moving again. It must be a mistake, I thought. I had done nothing wrong. It's a mistake.

It was hot and I was sweaty and the tape wasn't very secure on my face. It came off easily the second time; my face was wet from sweat and it just slipped off when I nudged it with my fingers. And it wasn't hard for me to get my hands out of the bag again as I had done before. I started to make noise, and I started to try to talk again, to get their attention. I wasn't calling for help any more – I knew there was no point in that. The people driving were the ones who had taken me. But I kept trying to talk. I kept trying to make noise for…well, I'm not really sure. In my mind I wanted answers, and I wanted to be heard. I wasn't just going to lie there in silence. After about twenty minutes or so I felt the car slow and I heard the handbrake noise again.

The boot opened again and the two of them were standing there, watching me. Then one of them leant in and lifted my head up, out of the bag, and propped it on the raised bit in the boot – the wheel arch. 'Thirsty,' I slurred. Then he poured water into my mouth. It was sparkling water. He poured it very carefully, taking his time, allowing me to have three sips. But that was enough. It was so hot in the boot, so I was grateful for anything. It was weird though – why would they give me water? Why would they care about me getting too hot? They were trying to keep me alive for something. My mind was whirring from the heat, from the drugs, from all the questions I had about what was happening to me.

Neither of them spoke to me. They didn't even speak to each other. It was all done in complete silence. After they had given me the water they undid the handcuffs round my wrists. Had they realised they had made a mistake? They didn't give me long to think about anything, as they then moved my arms back and behind me, now handcuffing my hands behind my back. They were very gentle, not rough, and they didn't hurt me when they moved my arms. The bottom half of my body was still in the bag but now my hands were cuffed behind me. They realised it was a struggle to put me fully back in the bag and do it up. I was now in a different position and not so easily fitted, or curled into, the bag.

Now my arms were behind me, and they allowed my shoulders to be out of the bag. That was such a relief – I wasn't going to be curled up in the bag any more – but the position I was in now, with my hands behind my back, meant I was lying on one arm and I was a lot more uncomfortable. When they first opened the boot I had been able to turn and face them, but now my arms were behind me I couldn't move. My shoulder and arm were hurting already from this new position, and even though the water had quenched my thirst it also made me want more. I was so hot. I was grateful I wasn't in my thick jacket but then I realised I wasn't the one who had removed it. What had happened? Why did they take my clothes off?

I didn't have a clue what had happened during that time, my last memory being of the man and the syringe. I closed my eyes. They had taken my clothes off. OK. Had I been raped? I think I would have known, wouldn't I? I think so. But if it hasn't happened yet, will it happen? I just didn't know what was going to happen…was I going to be raped or killed, or tortured? Would anyone know where I was? Would anyone find me? I had to concentrate but the air in the boot was hot and heavy and I was struggling to stay calm. They had put the tape back on my mouth again. I think they thought that, with my hands behind me, I wouldn't be able to peel it off.

They put the parcel shelf back and I could see something else go on top. A suitcase. It was a black suitcase, it was partly open and I could see it was empty. Why was there a suitcase? My mind then turned against me. This was for me. They would kill me and put me in the suitcase. The boot slammed shut and the car started to move. The radio went back on. It seemed louder than before. Were they trying to talk without me hearing?

The tape on my mouth didn't stay put for long. It was the same bit of tape. They hadn't replaced it with new stuff when they reapplied it. I stuck my tongue right out of my mouth and the tape came away easily. The waxy black bag was still covering the bottom half of me and it was a relief not to be fully inside its material prison.

It was probably about another half an hour later before the car stopped for the third time. I couldn't turn my head round to see what was happening, my handcuffed arms behind me keeping me in a fairly rigid position. I heard the boot open and then, before I realised what was happening, one of the men, now without a ski mask, jumped in and lay behind me. I was shocked. What the hell? Why was he in the boot? And why has he taken off his mask? He was lying next to me, trying to keep his long legs tucked into the small, now even more cramped, space. He had to lie facing the same way I was facing – there wasn't room otherwise – so it was like he was spooning me.

There wasn't time to process why he was suddenly next to me. As soon as the boot shut I took my chance to talk. The car engine started up and the car began to move. This man was now my companion for the journey and I wanted to get as much out of him as I possibly could. I wanted to know everything.

'What's happening?' I asked. 'Where am I?' I suppose I wasn't expecting him to reply, as there had been nothing but silence until now, but maybe if I was persistent he would talk; he would tell me something. Anything. And before I could ask again, he did.

'You not get hurt, don't worry,' he said, in broken English with an accent. He was softly spoken. And he was trying to reassure me. 'Nobody hurt you, I promise,' he said again. He wasn't whispering but he wasn't being overly loud.

'Where are we going?' I asked him. 'Where are you taking me?'

'I don't know,' he said. My mind was spinning. He didn't know? He was acting clueless. Why? Surely he knew where we were going.

'How can you not know where we're going?' I wanted answers and I wanted him to tell me.

'I don't know.'

I wasn't going to give up. He must know something, he could tell me something. 'Who is that driving then?' I persisted. I saw two guys, and I thought they must be friends or something. He was momentarily shocked. I could see he was taken completely by surprise at my question.

'What?! What?! No, I don't know who that is.'

'How can you not know who it is?' I was getting scared again now. 'How can you not know?'

That was the chilling part; he was trying to be nice and was trying to reassure me, but if he didn't know who the guy driving was, how could he know I would be safe and not hurt? How could he know?

I carried on asking: 'Is my luggage in the car? Where are my clothes? Will I get my flight tonight?' He kept saying, over and over, 'I don't know, I don't know.'

I started to cry. The realisation of everything that was happening just took over and I couldn't control it any longer. I was in tears.

'Don't cry, nobody hurt you, don't cry,' he said. He was trying to make me feel better. Did he feel sorry for me?

It didn't help. He didn't know anything or he wasn't telling me anything. The enormity of the situation hit me and I couldn't help it. I just lay there handcuffed in a bag in the boot of a car and let the tears come. I have been asked so many times, by interviewers, by friends, by TV presenters, what was going through my mind in those moments. To tell you the truth, my thoughts were so jumbled up in trying to make sense of everything, I couldn't even explain it if I tried. The tears were for me, for my mum, for my baby boy. I didn't know what was going to happen to me and I didn't know whether I would ever see them again. And those thoughts, that realisation, was unbearable.

CHAPTER 3

My living hell

*'"I don't know if you remember but I briefly
met you in Paris," he said. He was so calm and
sounded so normal.'*

The rest of the journey I spent with the man behind me
in the boot. Two bodies crammed into such a small space
meant it was extra hot and I couldn't stop crying. I was so
uncomfortable, and the handcuffs around my wrists behind
my back were so sore. I pleaded with the man in the boot
to undo them for me, just so I could lie with my hands and
arms in front of me. Just so I could be comfortable and not
have them forced behind me. I wasn't ever worried that he
was going to hurt me – I didn't think that was the point of
him getting in the boot. It was like he was there to reassure
me, calm me down.

'Just for now,' I sobbed. 'Please, they are so sore.' He

seemed to understand that I was in pain so he started knocking at the parcel shelf and the side of the boot.

He then started shouting 'Key! Key!' along with the banging and eventually the car stopped. I was grateful to this man behind me. He knew how to get the driver's attention and he wanted to try to help me, I thought.

The boot opened and the other man, the driver, who was still wearing a mask, passed him the keys. Neither of them said a word to each other and the driver just shut the boot again. The man behind me was able to unlock my handcuffs and I moved my arms in front of me. It was such a relief I can't tell you.

'Only for the journey,' said my boot companion. But that was fine with me. My right shoulder was still feeling a little numb but at least I could move it forward a bit now and not have it pulled back behind me. But my hair had got caught. I could feel, when I moved my head, a tugging – it was all tangled at the back and caught on something. I tried to pull it and pull it, and I was sure lots of my hair was coming out but it wasn't coming free. He helped me, he untangled it, and it came free in the end. All the movement of my head and my body to twist my hair free meant that my boob had become exposed. I wasn't wearing a bra under my bodysuit and I could feel his hand on my top, pulling it back over my boob. He was protecting my modesty, covering me up. I hadn't realised what had happened until I felt him tug the bodysuit back over my boob.

'Where are we?' I asked him again. 'What's happening?'

But he was clueless, or he was acting clueless. He didn't know, he said.

We probably travelled for another half an hour. I cried for the rest of that journey, silently. The tears would roll down my cheeks and mix in with the sweat from my face but at least I could wipe them away. I needed the toilet, I told the man behind me, but he didn't say anything. It's hard to describe the things I thought about when I was lying in that boot. I suppose the realisation hadn't quite sunk in. And I had so many unanswered questions. I would be released and I might even be able to get home on my flight that night. I would be home. I would see Mum and Ashton…no, no, I mustn't start thinking of them. If I let my mind go to them I wouldn't be able to think straight. I must just concentrate on what is happening now, what— I felt the car stop and the engine turn off, cutting off thoughts of my mum and son with it. The masked man came round and opened the boot and the unmasked man got out. That is who they were to me – masked guy and unmasked guy. I waited in the boot. The unmasked guy spoke.

'You'll have to wear the handcuffs again now,' he said. 'Or…' and he made an injection sign with his thumb, moving it up and down like he was clicking a pen. It was a warning.

Just the thought of being drugged again made my blood run cold and I held out my hands to show willingness. I wasn't going to cause trouble. I looked at the unmasked man and pleaded with my eyes: just please don't inject me again. The masked man put the handcuffs back on so my hands were in front of me and new tape was over my mouth. Then I was shuffled back inside the bag and zipped up. I had to curl myself round to fit into it. The darkness didn't scare me. I just wanted to know where we were going but that was impossible. I felt their hands on the bag as they lifted me up and out of the boot. I was being carried by both of them – I could tell one was near my head and one at the other end, near my legs. The hole that was my air hole was being covered by one of them too, so I couldn't see anything. At one point I felt like I was being tilted, like they were moving uphill. They put me down, very gently. They needed a break. It was hot in that bag. I could breathe OK there and then, but I started to panic that I might be in there for a long time… What if I was going to die in the bag? Almost as soon as I thought that, they put me down again and I heard a door unlocking. They picked me up and I felt hard floor underneath me as they put me gently down again. And then a loud slam.

They unzipped the bag. I went from complete darkness to a weak, artificial light and my eyes adjusted to the dim surroundings. The unmasked man told me to stand up. It was always him who spoke, never the masked man. He would point and direct but I never heard his voice. The unmasked guy told me to stand up again and I tried but I couldn't. The handcuffs were too tight on my ankles and I could only manage to half get up – to my knees – before I had to sit back down again on the floor. It was ice cold. 'I can't,' I said. I pointed to my ankles.

Unmasked guy came forward to unlock the cuffs from my ankles. He didn't take them off – perhaps he thought I would make a run for it – instead he loosened them. It was such a relief. I hadn't realised how tightly they were digging into me until they were loosened. Then he took the tape off my mouth and undid the handcuffs from my wrists.

'I need the toilet,' I told them. I looked at the unmasked man when I spoke. I didn't want to look at the other guy, he scared me. The masked man pointed to the stairs and the unmasked guy started walking over to them like he wanted me to follow him. My legs felt so unsteady that I thought I would fall down, but I slowly, steadily climbed the concrete stairs. It was tricky, not only because my muscles felt like they were working for the first time but also having my ankles chained meant I couldn't stretch that far. The stairs were right in front of me. They were of an open-plan design, no bannister or wall, just stairs going up.

They were grey and looked like stone or concrete. The kitchen. I was in the kitchen. I didn't look around too much or take everything in but I remember seeing a wooden table too. I can't remember what else, or if there was anything on the table. The masked man was watching me, in silence. His gaze was petrifying. I just wanted to follow unmasked guy to get away from him. He took me up the stairs and to a bathroom. Everywhere felt damp and cold. A musty, mouldy damp smell filled the air. He stood inside the bathroom as I went to the toilet, but I didn't care that he was there. I was more frightened of the masked man. This was the one who had been reassuring me; he had helped me in the boot. I could see the masked man by the doorway at the top of the stairs. He was watching me.

There was no bath in the bathroom, just a shower. I looked around as quickly as I could. I wanted to see and process everything. It wasn't dirty but it wasn't immaculate. There was just a shower, toilet and sink.

I finished in the toilet and unmasked man and masked man were both there. The masked man raised a hand and pointed over to a chest of drawers. There was a sleeping bag on the floor next to it. That is what he was pointing at. He was the one in control. He didn't speak but he didn't need to. He had power over the unmasked man. I had a sense he was the one in charge.

Did he want me to get in it? I walked over to it and bent down to try to find the zip. I tried to start unzipping it but masked man started shaking his head. So I just lay on top of it. I was shivering. I was just in my pink bodysuit and socks and all of a sudden I felt so exposed. The house felt really chilly and I started to shiver. I lay down on the sleeping bag and waited. Masked guy pointed at unmasked guy and then to the chest of drawers next to me. It was a silent direction for him to handcuff me to the chest of drawers, so he did.

He did my hands first. He took the handcuffs and locked one in place around my wrist. He then put the other one around the leg of the chest of drawers and then back around my other wrist. He then did the same with my ankles. He uncuffed one and wrapped it round the drawer leg and then back around my other ankle so I was attached to the furniture. The chest of drawers was as wide as I was long. I was stretched out on my side against it, on the sleeping bag. I still had no clue what was going on but I didn't ask any questions. I stayed silent. I couldn't move.

Once I was secured in place they both left the room. The entrance to the room had one of those beaded curtains that hang across door frames, and it clattered noisily as they walked through it. I looked around the small room. Apart from the chest of drawers the only other thing in there was a single bed. It was right next to where I was lying. It had a multi-coloured quilt on top of it. The colours looked too bright and cheerful for this room. They didn't match the dull, cold grey of the house.

I could hear them moving around downstairs and talking. It was in a different language but I could make out two voices. They weren't shouting or anything, just talking normally. That is all I can tell you about listening to them. I couldn't make out any words or vital bits of information. I told the police I heard only talking, just like I'm telling you now.

The unmasked man came back upstairs after twenty minutes or so. He sat cross-legged on the floor by my head. I studied his face. He had quite soft features and light-brownish hair. He didn't look like a monster. He didn't look like someone who would drug and kidnap a girl. He spoke quietly to me, making eye contact with me, and I heard him say in a soft voice that they had just been on the phone to the boss. The boss was furious, he said, because they had apparently got the wrong person. I can't tell you what that felt like. It was such a relief. I knew it! I knew it had all been just a big mistake.

'The boss is on his way,' he said.

'I have done nothing wrong. I knew it was a mistake,' I said. I had found my voice and I was so, so happy. His boss was obviously coming to release me.

'The boss is coming,' he said again, 'but I have to leave now for other job.' That wasn't good news. I didn't want to be left here with the masked man downstairs. I didn't want to be left alone with him; he scared me. His silence scared me.

'Please stay,' I asked. 'Please.' But he said he had to go. And that was that. He stood up and put fresh tape on my mouth and then left. I heard the beads clattering, and then silence. The next noise I heard was either a television or a radio, it was that sort of continuous sound.

The boss will come and set me free, I thought. I didn't think who this boss was or who he was the boss of. I just thought that soon, soon, I would be released. They had taken the wrong person. I would be home soon. Maybe I could even still catch my flight tonight. It was possible.

★ ★ ★

I waited for what seemed like ages on that sleeping bag. It was OK, I kept telling myself, they know it's a mistake now so I will have to be set free. I tried not to think about the masked man downstairs. I just wanted the boss to come and set me free so I could go home. I really wanted to go home. Time dragged on… I closed my eyes as I lay there but I was too anxious to drift off. I can sleep on the plane, I told myself. I can sleep when I'm safely on the plane.

Slam! I was jolted out of my thoughts by a door slamming.

The front door? Was this the boss? I heard raised voices, angry-sounding voices. I couldn't make out any words and it was another language but the voices were loud. And then – *Slam!* – another door closed. Had someone left? Who was here now? I couldn't sit up, I couldn't curl up; I just had to lie there and wait and see what was happening. After the second door slammed I heard one voice: one voice talking and pausing and talking again. The voice seemed angry, cross, loud… My senses were very acute as to what was taking place. When you are physically limited to listening, your whole mind focuses on every little clue. The voice seemed angry when it spoke. Then quiet. Then the angry voice again. He must have been on the phone, pausing for answers from the person on the other end of the line. It went on for about ten minutes and then there was silence. I waited. Had the conversation finished? After about five minutes I coughed loudly. I wanted the boss downstairs to know I was here, otherwise he couldn't help me. He needs to know I am here, I thought. Should I cough again?

I heard footsteps on the stairs and then the clicking and clattering of the doorway beads. A man I didn't recognise came into the room. He came over and pulled the tape off my mouth and then sat on the single bed next to me and started to talk. I strained my neck to look round at him. I was still handcuffed facing the chest of drawers. He saw that I was struggling and knelt down to undo the handcuffs around my hands. I could now twist myself round to see him.

'I don't know if you remember, but I briefly met you in Paris,' he said. He was so calm and sounded so normal. My mind was spinning. In Paris? I looked at him. He was clean-shaven, had mousy brown hair and was wearing a white T-shirt. He didn't look sinister or scary at all. Suddenly my memory clicked in. Skinny guy in Paris... sunglasses... Andre the photographer. And then everything fell into place. As soon as he mentioned Paris I knew: the cancelled photo shoot. It wasn't a mistake me being here. It was all set up to kidnap me.

'Andre? The photographer?' I whispered. It was him. I hadn't recognised him at first, as in Paris he was wearing those sporty-type sunglasses. He was just someone else I spoke to that day, no one significant. No one memorable.

He smirked. 'I'm definitely not a photographer.'

My heart sank. He was grinning in a horrible way. I knew I had been purposely captured. I didn't say anything. I couldn't speak at that point.

Andre started to talk and I just listened.

'Those stupid Romanians,' he said, 'they weren't meant to take you.'

Romanians? I thought. He continued: 'They can't understand English. Stupid Romanians. They couldn't understand the difference between must and mustn't.'

He was talking as if everything would make sense to me. He must have been talking about masked and unmasked guy.

'Can I just go home?' I asked him. 'I don't know what's happening. I don't know what's going on but can I just go now? If they weren't meant to take me...couldn't I just go home?'

He told me it wasn't that simple. 'You've already been advertised,' he said. 'You are for sale.'

CHAPTER 4

An auction for my life

*'"We can't upset the clients," he said.
"You have already been advertised."'*

My mum watches a lot of action films. She watches TV programmes about money laundering, drugs, sex trafficking. She watches too many movies with that stuff in. I haven't even seen *Taken*, the Liam Neeson film that everyone seems to have watched, but I knew what sex trafficking was from what I've heard on TV, although my knowledge was limited. I suppose it was probably for the best that I didn't have too much of an idea of the details – or the horrific depths behind its meaning.

'Your advert,' he said, 'has caused huge interest. The auction for you is in five days' time, on Sunday. The starting price is three-hundred thousand US dollars.'

I couldn't take it all in. I didn't understand what was

happening. I was told they had taken the wrong person, so why was I suddenly for sale? He was talking all the time these thoughts were going through my mind, like it was the most usual thing in the world.

'It's not up to me now,' he was saying. 'It's other people's decision. But while I'm alive you're not going anywhere. But it's not up to me.' He made it sound like he was defending me. It wasn't a threat; he was trying to help me. But it was out of his control.

I didn't understand.

'But you are the boss, aren't you? The other man, he told me the boss is coming, that is you, isn't it?' I just wanted to understand what was happening. I wanted to know what was going on.

He was acting like it wasn't his decision, like it was other people's decision now. That was scary. Why can't I just go home? I was shocked but I wasn't getting angry. I had questions, lots of questions. 'Who is the boss? Why can't I go home like he said?'

I looked at Andre. I was speaking normally to him. He didn't answer my questions, he just said: 'You're taking this really well. The other girls, they're screaming and crying…'

His sentence hung in the air. He said it so casually. Other girls? I didn't know what to say to that. So this isn't the first time, I thought. I'm not special. I'm just another girl.

He kept talking. I was stunned into silence. I lay there listening as he told me about Paris. He explained he had cancelled the shoot. He told me that the Romanians, the people who took me, had showed him a photo of me. They always show him the photos of the girls they are taking, he said. So casually. Like it was nothing. They showed him the photo and then he went on my Instagram account, he said. And he saw a photo of me and Ashton. It went against the rules, he was telling me. It's against the rules to take such a person. So he cancelled Paris. And then he said he sent them an email telling them, 'This girl mustn't be taken'.

My mind was in overdrive. I lay there, handcuffed to the furniture, listening to him telling his side of events in a tone of voice that sounded completely blasé. He was just saying everything so frankly, so openly, as if he was merely passing the time of day.

'Why…why did you rebook me?' I asked. 'Why did you tell me to go to the studio if I wasn't to be taken? I don't understand.' If he was Andre, and he cancelled me because I shouldn't have been taken in Paris, then why did he email Phil to rebook in Milan? Why would he rebook me if he said I mustn't be kidnapped?

'I know nothing about these emails,' he said. 'They were using my Andre account. They thought there was a typing mistake. They thought "mustn't take" should have been "must" take. They thought it was a typo.'

Simple as that. Like it was a silly mistake. That it didn't actually involve me – a person. He kept talking. He told me he had just driven over from his holiday in Rome and that we were no longer in Italy. 'I can't tell you where we are. We are in a remote place. There are no shops or people for miles,' he said.

He was trying to scare me.

'I have come because I have seen you. I have seen the advert on the website; you are advertised.' He told me when he realised it was me he was furious. 'What website?' I asked.

Was I taking all of this in? It's hard to say. He was saying everything so clearly, so matter-of-factly. I didn't understand what was happening, but he was talking to me like he was explaining something so simple. Then he mentioned a name: Black Death.

'I'm not having this. I'm strongly against this. I'm furious. But this rule is something that Black Death are flexible on,' he continued. I was trying to follow and keep up and process what he was saying. He went on to tell me that Black Death was a criminal organisation, a gang that kidnapped young women and sold them online to wealthy Arabs. He said he was known as 'MD' in the gang. That was his name. Andre wasn't real.

I will refer to Andre as 'MD' from now on. He was MD to me all the time I was held captive. I wasn't to find out his real identity until later on, when he was under arrest. Only then would I find out his real name was Lukasz Herba, and that he was a Polish national. I saw it on a police document a few days after my release.

'Why can't I go home?' I asked

'If you were pregnant you would be home straight away.' He looked at me. 'But the clients have already been asked if they mind that you are a young mother and they don't care. Black Death are flexible on this. Mothers should not be taken and neither should pregnant girls but sometimes it happens.'

So that's why he had to fight for this decision to release me. It wasn't up to him, he told me. It was up to the people above him. Apparently he was a 'Level 12' operative of a twenty-layer mafia, Black Death. He was boasting as he said this. He never hesitated. He didn't stop to think about anything. Everything he was telling me was said so matter-of-factly, so naturally, that I believed what he was saying. He talked like he was confident about all the answers to everything I asked.

I had heard the argument downstairs. Did I hear the words 'must' and 'mustn't' being said on the phone? Perhaps I did. This must be true…it made sense.

'So, what happens now?' I asked him. 'When do they decide about me?'

'We can't upset the clients,' he said. 'You have already been advertised.' But he wanted to help me, he said. He told me it was a mistake my being there, but the money needed to be paid.

'What do your family have to offer?' he asked me.

'We don't have anything,' I said. It was just Mum and me at home, and we didn't have that sort of money. He carried on. What about Phil, my agent? he asked. I said Phil didn't have that kind of money either. He wanted the names of three people who might be able to help; who could lay their hands on the kind of money they were looking for.

He stood up. 'I will give you a while to think.' And then he left. I tried to think. I was trying to process everything that he had been saying. This was good, wasn't it? There was still hope if the money could be paid.

He came back after about fifteen minutes and I gave him three names. They were just people I thought of on the spot, under pressure. Rory McCarthy, who is a close friend of mine, who would help if he could; Dave Reed, a celebrity agent who does the PR for *Sixty6* magazine, a publication I have modelled for. And Paul Chaplin, the owner of *Loaded* magazine. I was hoping that one of them would be able to help. He wrote the names down. He said he would email them to Phil so he could get the money together before Sunday – the day the auction started for my life.

He stood up to leave the room. He told me he was going to send the emails. I asked him if he would call my mum to let her know I was alive. He shook his head. 'Noooo,' he said. It was a really long, drawn-out response. He said he would email Phil to do it. I gave him my mum's number. But it wasn't until later I realised I had given him the wrong number. I always give my mum my old handsets when I've finished with them, so I gave him an old number. He told me he would have to go outside and email. The house was in such a remote location that you could only get a signal at the bottom of the hill. I just nodded. I didn't question it. At least now Phil would raise the alarm and people would start looking for me. Please, please, please, I thought, please someone help me.

I couldn't see whether or not it was dark outside by this point because all the windows had the shutters pulled across them. But I guessed it must have been late in the afternoon. Phil would see his email and raise the alarm. I was sure of it. I started to shiver. I was lying on top of the sleeping bag and I couldn't get in it because of my handcuffs. So I just lay there. I could hear MD wandering around. I heard the beads clatter when he came in and he gave me a bottle of water and three books. He piled them in front of me.

'They are the only English books I have,' he said. I didn't even look to see what they were. It was such a normal, everyday thing, to read, and yet I was lying, handcuffed, semi-naked and up for sale online. I don't understand why he thought I would ever want to read those books.

He went out again. Then after about fifteen minutes he came back. He brought me a red blanket. It had a fleecy back to it and some sort of white pattern. I was so grateful for it, as I was really cold on the damp floor. I hadn't asked for it, or the water. I was doing everything I was being told. I wasn't causing a fuss, so I guess he thought I was worthy of some basic comfort.

He sat on the bed and talked to me again. He enjoyed talking and telling me about Black Death and, at that stage, I didn't want to know what they were. I was struggling with processing any of what he was telling me, but I didn't want to make trouble. If I did everything I was told, if he had just emailed Phil, maybe I would be home soon, I thought.

So I listened. It was just him and me now, he said. He told me he had sent the two Romanians to Berlin, to the Black Death headquarters. They would have to go on trial and pay back the money they got for taking me. They shouldn't have taken me and so they would stand trial. The organisation doesn't take disobedience lightly, he said. 'The driver would have to stand trial too, for not doing his job properly.' He made it all sound so official.

'Black Death are a criminal organisation,' he continued. 'It isn't just trafficking. They do drugs, assassinations, everything,' he said. They were part of the 'deep web' – that is what he called it. There was the normal web, the dark web and then the deep web. Then he talked about what he did in Black Death, what his role was. He was an assassin, he told me. He would be ordered to kill people. He would kill them by poisoning them. It was his way, not too messy. Besides, he said, no one investigates a death by heart attack.

And then he told me about kidnapping and what happens to girls who are taken. He spoke so calmly, so matter-of-factly. It wasn't a big deal to him, it was business. I listened. The girls, after they're taken, he said, get flown to Saudi Arabia, where men use them. And when they get bored they pass the girls around their families, to the uncles, friends, brothers. And then, eventually, after a few months, they feed them to their pet tigers. Or kill them in other ways.

I couldn't take it all in but it sounded like you didn't make it out alive. If I didn't raise the money, I would die. How do you process that? How did I process it? I honestly couldn't tell you. It was the stuff of nightmares – a fear so horrific that you can't think about it. It doesn't seem real now I'm writing this in the comfort of my own home. But then, on the cold floor, in a dark room, handcuffed to a chest of drawers…everything was real. I was so scared.

I didn't know what to say to him. I just lay there. This could be me. If I didn't raise the money, that would be it. If that was the rule and he wasn't the highest member in Black Death, and couldn't stop it, it would be me. He said he wanted to help me but he didn't have the overall say. But he was willing to try to help. He said he would do everything he could to help me.

And then, 'I will even pay some of the money.' I wasn't sure what I was hearing. Was he trying to help me? Was he willing to help pay for my release? Did he feel guilty that I was captured? He wasn't allowed to pay for the whole thing, he said, even if he wanted to, so I had to raise some of the money. I was grateful to him. I believed him. I trusted what he was telling me. He was trying to help me.

★ ★ ★

It seemed he liked to chat. He would tell me about Black Death and then he would leave the room. Like he wanted me to dwell on it, to take it all in. Sometimes when he left I would just lie there and close my eyes. I wasn't sleeping; the beads always made too much noise when he passed the door or came back in. For the rest of my life I will remember those beads across the doorway. I will never be able to go through or see or hear beads like that ever again without going back to that house.

I was facing the chest of drawers but I could tell whenever he came into the room, thanks to the noise of the beads. One time he came and asked me if I wanted anything from the shop. He made a big deal of it being so far away.

'Toothbrush and toothpaste?' I asked him. He nodded. I am obsessed with my teeth. I would brush them five times a day at home, so this was incredible. It was like a sense of victory – surely if there was no hope, he wouldn't be trying to help me.

Another time he came in and brought me a plate of food. He put it down on the floor next to me. It had honey on it, which was about the only thing I recognised. I didn't touch any of it. I wasn't hungry anyway but what he had told me played on my mind. Had he poisoned it? Was this a plan to kill me? I was overcome with exhaustion. I wanted to nap, maybe, and be alert, but whether it was the drugs still in my system or the enormity of the situation, I slept. That first night, my first night held captive, I didn't put up any sort of fight. I didn't force myself to stay awake or try to concoct an escape plan in my head. I was on the floor, handcuffed to a chest of drawers in an unknown country and with a man who was going to sell me to the highest bidder. My mind just shut down then and I closed my eyes and I slept.

CHAPTER 5

Somebody help me

'I asked to go to the toilet a couple more times and he let me go whenever I needed it. I didn't actually always need to go; it was just a break to be able to stand up and walk before going back to lie down again to be handcuffed.'

I heard the beads clattering and opened my eyes. The chest of drawers I was facing was raised slightly off the floor and I could see underneath. Dust, dirt...this wasn't a dream. I wasn't waking up to the smile of my curly-haired boy. I wasn't snuggled under the warm duvet in my bedroom, listening to Nylah's howling downstairs. I let my mind drift to home and closed my eyes again. What would I be doing if I was at home now? I would be on the flight to Ibiza. Or I would be there by now. The excitement of buying those bikinis seemed like a lifetime ago now. Why is that?

Why does time trick you? I felt like I had been here, in this nightmare, for ever. I felt like I had been out of the 'real' world for too long already, and yet it was only a day. This was my second day in this place, this house. Would I ever see my house again? I knew I shouldn't think like that but I couldn't help it. I had until Sunday, the day of the auction ending, to know my fate. What then?

MD hadn't appeared in the room but the beads made a noise every time he walked past so I knew he was up. He wasn't angry, he wasn't mean... Would he be able to help? I was desperate to know if Phil had replied to his email. I was hoping Phil would let MD know that the police were searching for me and that there was no point keeping me hostage as I would be found soon, or that someone had seen me being taken and the police were tracking the car. Or that the money had been paid and I would be free to go. The plate of food was still lying by my head and the smell was making me feel sick.

There wasn't any air in the room and it was all musty. The shutters were still closed; they hadn't been opened since I had arrived and I suspected they probably never would be. The lights stayed on all the time, a strong, artificial light. I couldn't tell you what time it was. Morning? Had I slept long? The effects of the drugs must have still been in my system the previous night or the gravity of the situation would have been too overwhelming. I remember feeling so exhausted. I think I slept on and off most of the night. I know it seems so trivial, but I was always used to knowing everything that was going on from my phone – even just down to the time – that I felt lost without it. I was always on my phone – checking my Instagram account, checking messages, looking at photos. And now, nothing. It wasn't like I needed it, it just felt strange and I felt adrift, apart from the normal world. My life was so different already. But did it matter? What mattered now was getting home. What mattered now was being home. Being safe.

★ ★ ★

According to MD, we weren't in Italy. That is what he had told me last night. So where were we? I tried to imagine all the countries we might now be in but then I realised that was probably futile. I had no idea how I had got into the boot and therefore no idea what had happened to me. We could have been travelling for hours before I woke up. In the middle of nowhere.

'No one is around. We are in a remote place…' His words echoed in my head as I shuffled myself onto my back so that my arms were now at a slight angle across the top of my head.

However uncomfortable the handcuffs were, at least I didn't have to have tape across my mouth any more. Is that why he removed the tape? Because it wouldn't matter if I screamed or shouted, no one would hear me anyway if we were so isolated. If we weren't in Italy, I thought, maybe the police wouldn't ever find me. If they were looking at the studio in Milan, and I was now hundreds of miles away in another country, they might never find me.

The sleeping bag hadn't provided much padding that

night and my shoulder and back were aching from lying on the cold hard floor. And there was that horrid musty smell. I could hear cows mooing. That was strange but, in a weird way, comforting. Cows nearby…maybe there was a farm nearby too? A farmer?

He came through the beads and spoke to me. He sat down on the bed opposite and told me he had gone to feed the cows. This was his property, and he had nineteen other properties in remote locations where he had to do all this stuff, he said. Then he went away again. I lay there. There wasn't much else I could do. He would come in and talk for a bit, probably for no more than about twenty minutes or so, go away again and then come back. Sometimes I could hear him doing stuff downstairs, other times I would hear the door shut and I thought to myself, perhaps he is feeding the cows. Perhaps he is checking emails.

The next time he came in, I decided to ask him. I couldn't bear it any longer. 'What's happening?' I said. 'Has Phil emailed you back?'

He told me that Phil had sent him an email and all it said was 'received'. I couldn't believe it. 'Received'! That sounded like he was dismissing me, like a business email. He didn't care, I thought. Surely he would have reported it to the police. He must have alerted the police. I kept thinking about my mum. She would be out of her mind with worry.

MD was shocked that Phil sounded like he didn't care. He then told me that his boss in Black Death, 'CK', might consider releasing me if my family could pay 'whatever they could afford'. He said he felt sorry for me and that he would try to help pay some money too to make things right. He told me money was not an issue for him; he could easily pay it all back, but Black Death wouldn't allow that. 'It wouldn't be fair to the other clients,' he said. I didn't question why he was trying to help. I just believed everything so completely.

I needed to go to the toilet, I said. And without a word he came over and took the handcuffs off my feet and my wrists. It was such a wonderful feeling, standing up and stretching my legs. I felt a bit like Bambi at first, not totally trusting my legs to work as they needed to even for that short walk to the bathroom. I followed him and made my way to the toilet to sit down. He stood in the doorway but didn't look at me. Then, when I was finished, I started walking back. I wanted to savour each movement, each step, but I was only delaying the inevitable. He handcuffed me back to the chest of drawers.

I asked to go a couple more times and he let me go whenever I needed to. I didn't actually always need to go, it was just a break to be able to stand up and walk before going back to lie down again to be handcuffed. I didn't overuse the toilet card though; it wasn't like I was asking to go every five minutes.

In the afternoon I'd used the toilet and was walking back to the sleeping bag to lie down again when he spoke.

'You can have half of the bed if you want to.'

I turned round to look at him. He was looking at me in complete seriousness.

'You'd be an idiot to try and escape now,' he said. 'You stay in this room. Now, you know I'm trying to help you and that we are not even in Italy. We are in a remote location. And it would be the instant death penalty if you tried to escape. Black Death would administer the death penalty. You can't go downstairs.'

Do as he says or I'm killed. Why would I try to do anything but what he says? I hadn't thought about trying to escape at that point, and I wasn't going to now. I was completely numb with fear. My life wasn't in my hands; if I tried to leave I would be dead. There was so much fear growing inside me that I couldn't speak. I just nodded.

The bed was near the bathroom. So I followed him and saw the double bed in front of me. Half of it was covered with a yellow blanket and he had put my red blanket on the other half. I know this might sound strange, but it was such a relief to see a bed. My back was hurting and I couldn't face another night on that cold hard floor. It felt more human, more normal, to be on a bed. And I wouldn't be handcuffed either, I thought. I couldn't see anywhere where he could handcuff me to the bed, so in my mind that was a step in the right direction.

But how? Did it mean I had a bit more freedom? I was too scared to do anything. He had warned me not to go downstairs. I was scared he had set up a camera to spy on me or that if I tried to escape he would just kill me there and then, so I didn't even try.

Did I worry that I would be sharing a bed with a man who, at that time, I thought of as being my saviour? No. The media have made such a big deal about me sharing a bed with my 'kidnapper'. But to me, at that time, he was trying to help me. He wasn't my 'kidnapper' until I had been released and knew the truth. He spoke to me about the rules for the girls who are kidnapped. If they get raped or touched by their captors, the captors face the death penalty. If they touch the girls it devalues them, he said. I know it was only words but I trusted him. I sort of knew he wouldn't try anything. He took everything so seriously. Virgins sell for the most, he continued. Over a million US dollars. The girls were always aged between fourteen and twenty, so I was one of the oldest.

I went round to my side of the bed...my side, the side where my blanket was. It wasn't the floor. I had to get through this until Sunday. If I didn't have to sleep on the floor I could do this, I told myself.

Apart from the bed there was a clock, too, which made me feel a little more in control. With no natural light anywhere in the house, it was impossible to tell what time of day it was, but now I had a clock to look at. There was also a wardrobe in the room. It was quite an old-looking wardrobe and I could see the door was slightly open. I looked closely. It seemed there were some full black bin bags in there, spilling out slightly. I wasn't going to look in them or go near the wardrobe. To be honest, I didn't want to know what was in them.

I lay down on the bed. He sat down on his side and then moved his legs round so he was sitting on the bed, his back against the wall. The fact that he was still with me in the room meant that he was in one of his talkative moods. I had come to sense how he was, how he acted, when he wanted to talk and chat, and I would listen. Mostly it was him talking and me listening. If my recall of these events comes across as strangely unemotional, it's because, at the time, that was the only way I could process it. I couldn't associate what was happening to me with stuff he would talk about. 'Other girls' he spoke of were just that, 'other girls'. I couldn't picture myself as one of them.

★ ★ ★

He talked and I listened. He told me more about how Black Death operated, and how they chose and took girls. It was very simple, he said: they would take three or four girls a week. Virgins were extra value. They would never take girls from Britain; they would always operate in eastern European countries, he said.

I had questions, lots of questions, and it seemed to me that we were having a conversation. My questions were always answered and never ignored. I suppose that is why I thought everything he told me was true. Everything was answered, without pause, without hesitation.

'How would you take a girl, then, if she wasn't a model? How would you set it up?' I asked.

'Easy,' he said. They would be talking to girls in nightclubs or bars and then would ask them to go outside to chat. 'They would go for low-profile girls,' he said. 'The ones who don't tell their parents where they are going.' If they came they would then be loaded into a van.

He was boasting, yet saying it so casually. They would then hold the girls for a week, put them up for auction and then transport them to the Middle East, he said. Put them on a jet and land in an isolated spot. Any secluded piece of land.

He said he never normally did this, the actual guarding of a girl. He was too high up in Black Death to do the actual watching. He was sometimes aware of which girls were being taken, but he never normally had this type of interaction.

Did that make me feel special? Not really. He then went on to tell me that if I had been a bitch about anything, if I was screaming and shouting, he would have just got the Romanians to look after me. And I would still be handcuffed too. And if they were in charge, I wouldn't even be allowed to go to the toilet uncuffed. That's how bad the conditions were. He was making me feel grateful. It made me feel like I was doing something right.

★ ★ ★

And so that is how the rest of the day was spent. I would listen and sometimes ask questions. I didn't get anything to eat, though. He had moved the plate of food he'd brought the previous night into this new bedroom and the smell was horrible. I wasn't going to touch any of it. But he did give me water, a litre bottle of water. The seal was unbroken, so I knew he couldn't have poisoned it.

A while later, I asked if I could go to the toilet. I wasn't handcuffed to anything so it wasn't like I couldn't just get up myself and go, but he was still in control. I didn't feel like I could suddenly take myself off to the bathroom – I didn't want to upset him, or show him disrespect. He told me the next day I didn't have to ask him any more; he could see the toilet from the bedroom so there was no need for him to stand and watch me. For now, though, I still asked and he gave his permission.

Was it strange going to sleep on a bed next to a stranger who was keeping me prisoner? The sleeping arrangement was the least of my problems, if I'm honest. There wasn't a lot to it. He would turn over and sleep his side, while I would face the other way and sleep my side. In that situation, in that house, it was what it was. I was wrapped up in my red blanket, the fleecy side next to my skin, trying to keep warm. I wasn't freezing but I was still just in my bodysuit and, because I hadn't been moving about, the coldness crept in through my skin to my bones more than I was used to. I wrapped the blanket around me that night, hoping to have enough to put round my head, over the pillow, but it wasn't that big. I wanted to cover as much skin as I could, not just from the cold but because of the mosquitoes I'd seen buzzing around. And the bugs I could see on the bed. Tiny little insects on the thin sheet on top of the mattress. Well, it wasn't a sheet exactly, more like a thin covering. I put my blanket down on top of that and wrapped myself in the blanket to act like a duvet or a sleeping bag.

★ ★ ★

I had lots of bites, small red, itchy spots on my legs and arms that made my skin burn but – and I hope this doesn't sound crazy – it made me feel alive. I wasn't just an item up for auction, a thing to be sold…I was human. To the insects at least I was a normal person and, yes, it was uncomfortable to be bitten but it wasn't like it was unbearable. The first night, on the floor when I was looking at the bottom of the chest of drawers, I was looking for spiders, for cockroaches, for bugs. Back in the UK I was so scared of spiders. I hated them. Of course, that was then, when only a tiny spider would terrify me. What on earth could scare me about an insect or spider now, after what I'd been through? This was fear on another scale and, in this situation, I wasn't scared of six- or eight-legged creatures any more. So that's why the insect bites didn't bother me. I didn't want to lie on the bed and feel them crawl over me, but if I kept the blanket wrapped tightly around me I could try to get some sleep and not let them bother me.

MD went out to do his nightly email check. That would be a routine for him, three times a day. Morning, afternoon and late at night. He would go out and then report on what was happening. When he came up after his nightly check he had got changed. He came up and lay on the bed.

He controlled the lights. He would turn them on and off and, as soon as they went off, the house was thrown into complete darkness. It was a relief not to have that artificial light on all the time. I wasn't scared of the dark. I didn't need to be scared of it; what was happening to me was scary enough. He rolled over and that was that. I think he said goodnight. He fell asleep before me. I could hear his breathing become heavier and he would get that twitchy leg thing, where his leg would move suddenly but not wake him up.

It was like he wasn't even on the bed next to me. He kept to his side and I lay on mine, trying to fall asleep. It wasn't easy. This was when my mind tried to piece together everything he had told me during the day. At no point did I think, I could make a run for it, or I *should* make a run for it. There was no point thinking about escaping.

I often get asked about this in interviews. I think certain TV people want me to say that I was plotting a daring escape plan. Or that I tried to climb out of the window or something. But the point is this – I was just too scared. I wasn't being tortured. I believed MD was trying to help me, and all I wanted to do was get home to my little boy, my mum and Nylah. That was it. Nothing else mattered. I would have done anything to just be at home with my mum. Before all of this, before I was there and I was normal, I would sometimes find being at home a bit boring. I would dream of exploring new places or seeing the world, having some excitement. But in that damp bedroom, alone on the bed with a strange man, wrapped in a thin blanket, with no food and fearing for my life, I just wanted home more than anything else in the world.

★ ★ ★

I started to cry then. It was time for me to have a bit of a release, let the enormity of the situation hit me. And it did. I would never let him see me cry; I would always wait for him to go to sleep before my cheeks became wet and I would allow myself to think the worst. This wasn't the worst. This was OK, I could survive without eating, without washing, being isolated... I could survive this, but the unknown – that is what I couldn't face up to. On Sunday the auction for my life would begin. If I wasn't saved, if Phil didn't email to say he had the money, if the police never found me, if MD's boss didn't allow him to help me… Then my future was, and I don't use this word lightly, hell. There would be no other way to describe it. I would be in hell and then I would be fed to tigers or killed another way. My life would be over. I couldn't help thinking the worst at night. It was natural, to think of the worst possible outcomes. The what-ifs would drift into my mind and I would long for such normal everyday things. I just wanted to see my mum, to see my son, to see my dog. It made me realise what was important.

I know some people say crying is a good release, and strong people are allowed to cry too, but ever since I was a little girl I have never liked anyone seeing me cry. Mum has told me I have always been like it. I don't show emotion. Not just crying – I find it hard to show emotion in general. If someone tells me a shocking piece of news, I won't know how to react. I have always been like that, she says. When I was little I had a friend who would cry at everything and anything but I wasn't like that at all. I broke something at my mum's friend's house once and I laughed after it happened. Not because I found it funny; I just didn't know how to react, she said. She took me home and it wasn't until I was home that I started to cry. My mum's friend was shocked that I had laughed, as she thought that meant I had done it on purpose and didn't care. My mum had to explain.

So crying myself to sleep every night, without him seeing,

was the bit of control I had. I would often be awake two or three hours after he had gone to sleep, with the thoughts in my head and the tears on my cheeks, but that was my time. Sleep would come eventually, I knew it would, and by then I was ready to welcome it. I had gone through everything in my mind and sleep now was welcome.

CHAPTER 6

Alone

*'He sat on the bed and explained what
Black Death would do in the run-up to an auction
for other kidnapped girls.'*

I could hear the cows mooing – a strange sound to wake up to. Then my arm started to itch from a fresh insect bite, and I scratched it until my arm felt like it was on fire. I opened my eyes. I couldn't tell what time it was but the lights were on, the horrible artificial lights, not natural light, so I knew he was up. The window shutters, which were covering the door-sized window, shut out any sign of natural light. It is strange, waking up and your brain not registering what time of day it is by the light outside. That smallest little thing, that simple pleasure of seeing daylight, was suddenly something I longed for and realised I had taken for granted just a few days ago. Day three. My third day in the house. I knew it was Thursday and that meant there were only three days until I 'went up for auction' on Sunday.

I lay there waiting for MD to come back and let me know what news he had. His morning email check was done first thing. He 'went down the mountain' for better signal, he said. I was trying to imagine where we were – high up on a mountain, surrounded by cows and nothing else, it seemed.

★ ★ ★

Waiting for him to come with news of my fate was a pretty desperate experience. At this stage, I didn't know what to expect when he came back. I looked for clues in his face but he didn't give anything away.

I waited in silence. He knew I would be waiting to hear and told me as soon as he walked in that Phil hadn't emailed him back. He was in constant contact with his boss, CK, though, he said. 'No progress,' he told me. 'We wait for Phil.'

He and CK were waiting for Sunday, the auction. The starting price for me had attracted lots of interest, he told me again. It made me feel sick to my stomach. Please, Phil, I silently begged, please, please do something.

He sat on the bed and explained what Black Death would do in the run-up to an auction for other kidnapped girls. They hold them for a week before the sale date, he said. It gives them time for a doctor to come and check that the girl doesn't have an STI and isn't pregnant, he explained. It was all so matter-of-fact and so cold. These were people, this was me! I was screaming in my head, but said nothing.

He kept saying he was going to do all he could to help

and, because he hadn't been violent or aggressive to me, I believed him. When he asked if I wanted a shower, it was like he was trying to show me I could trust him. There would be no doctors coming to check me over. It was a mistake that I had been taken in the first place, so he was showing that I would be treated in a civil manner.

I was so grateful when he offered me a shower. I felt such a rush of excitement. It was something so simple, having a wash, but it made me feel human again. At home I'm super OTT about germs and I would have multiple baths a day. It was just something I did – I like to be clean, it was just part of the daily routine for me. This was wonderful. He went out of the bedroom and came back a few minutes later with an old T-shirt and pair of boxer shorts for me. They were clean, although well-worn, but in that moment they could have been a brand-new outfit with the tags on, such was the joy of seeing something fresh to wear. I'd thought I would have to put my bodysuit and socks back on, which were now grubby and smelt of stale sweat and dried fear.

I went into the bathroom and he told me to keep the door open. There was a shower curtain, though, and as soon as I turned on the shower and let the water run through my hands I actually didn't care who saw me. The warmth of the water, the cleansing of my skin, was glorious. I felt so happy. I stood under that shower and felt relief. In that moment I closed my eyes and I could have been at home, I could have been anywhere. This was normal, an everyday event in my old life, but now it was like the most special occasion in the world.

I tried to untangle my hair but it was so thick and matted nothing really helped. I didn't have a hairbrush but I did see some shampoo on the side and used that to wash it and my fingers to try to comb it through.

Did I think he would try to come in and watch me? No. I didn't think that was his game. He seemed too professional to do that. He was too high up in Black Death. He was in a position of authority – not the boss, but he wasn't just a rough kidnapper. He was in charge of people and I thought he would have some sort of decency code to abide by. He had never come across like that so far. He had always stuck to his side of the bed.

I let the water run and run. I tried to prolong the shower for as long as possible. I just wanted to stay and let it wash over me until I could wash away everything that had happened. I felt so grateful.

I came out of the shower feeling like a different person. I was still here, I was alive and I felt, for the first time, that I might be OK. Funny how a shower can change that about you! There was a towel on the side. It looked clean enough, so I picked it up. I moved close to the wall to get changed, so he couldn't see me. I was out of his line-of-sight from the bedroom. It wasn't until I was dressed that I came out of the bathroom. For the first time since I had been taken, I felt human again.

The sense of independence I had from having a shower in relative privacy was short-lived. He reminded me when I came out that 'here and there', the bathroom and bedroom, were the only places I could go. I went back over to the bed and lay down. There wasn't anything else to do now. I knew I couldn't go downstairs. Even if I crept down there when he was doing his email checks, then what? What if he had set up a camera as a trap, to spy on me, and then saw me deliberately disobey him? I just wanted to do what I was told and not try anything that would make him or Black Death angry.

It was as if, when I lay down on the bed, it was his cue to start talking. It passed the time, listening to him talk, and whether he was telling me about himself or Black Death, he seemed to enjoy speaking, so I just listened. The conversations he had with me in those first two days were very minimal, necessary. Now, it seemed, he was still very formal but was opening up more. And I just lay there, listening to my captor speak.

★ ★ ★

His talk would always revolve around Black Death in one way or another, and now he was telling me how he got involved. He told me he used to be in the army and that he enjoyed being a soldier. Then someone introduced him to Black Death. They told him about the criminal organisation and how he could start at a higher level than most people as he already had a good base of military experience. He said he felt honoured to be asked, especially as he wouldn't have to go into the organisation at the bottom. Most people start from the bottom, Level 1, he said, and Black Death goes up to Level 20. That's the highest. The Romanians who took me, he said, they do the kidnapping. They were only Level 1. So was the courier. He himself was able to join Black Death at Level 8, thanks to his army experience, and in five years of being with them, had made it to Level 12. He said he didn't deal with the taking of the girls; he wasn't physically involved with any of that.

His level duties did, however, involve dealing with assassinations. He was saying it so casually, like it was normal. That was what was so scary. He could have been telling me he stacked shelves in Tesco, the way he spoke about it. He killed people for a living.

I asked questions but I can't remember exactly what. I suppose I was intrigued. He told me how he killed people – his technique, as it were.

It was quite simple, he explained. He would use poison or rifles. And he had killed many people. He had killed in the thousands, he said. He said he didn't get emotional over it; he did it so regularly, he said. It didn't affect him.

Talking about killing made him seem like a robot, very mechanical, but then he started talking about the kidnapping and the sex trafficking and he became angry. He said he had no sympathy for the girls who were kidnapped. It was their fault for being stupid and naïve and getting themselves into such situations.

I didn't quite understand. 'Why is it their fault?' I ventured to ask.

'Why don't they check and find out about the places they are going to?' he said. 'Why don't they do the proper checks on places, on people, on venues?' In my case, he was insinuating it was through my agent not doing the proper checks. But it was obvious he was lacking sympathy for these girls who went to places far from home that they didn't know anything about.

I didn't say anything. But it made me think the guy was cold and heartless. How could it be our fault? But why, if he was so angry with the girls, did he care so much about the young mother rule? Why was that rule so important to him? Why was he trying to help me so much? As if he knew what I was thinking, he answered my question.

He said it happened to his mum. He said he would have wanted this – someone to help her – when he was young. I was stunned. I didn't know what to say…had his mum been kidnapped? Had his mum been taken from him when he was a young boy? Is this why the rule was so significant to him? I didn't know if that was true but I could only go on what he told me. He didn't elaborate, he didn't give me any more details, he just said: 'Because it happened to my mum, I would want the same.'

I didn't question him. I didn't want to push him.

He would answer everything I asked on Black Death. He had moved on to telling me what he earned and what he did and went into so much detail I couldn't not believe him. He told me how much he had earned while working for them for five years – fifteen million dollars, he said. And money was no object for him; he had plenty of money, it wasn't ever a concern. That is why, he said, he was willing to pay the majority of my ransom. He had no hesitation. He told me he didn't normally wear the clothes he was wearing – jeans and a T-shirt – he said he normally wore very nice suits. Tailored suits, he said. That was him trying to impress me, I thought.

If I had a rich family they would have bought me back, he said. This is what other parents had done, apparently. He said sometimes parents watched the auctions when they went live and bought their girls back. And sometimes, if the girls taken came from Monaco or smaller countries, the governments of those countries would pay to save them. I don't know why he told me all this but he did. Was he boasting? I guess he was a little cocky about the simplicity of it all. There was never any hesitation when he spoke. I never doubted what he said.

★ ★ ★

The rest of my day was spent listening to him talk. His boss was called CK and this was the only operative he knew above him. You only know one level higher than your own. So while Black Death goes up to Level 20, MD knows only CK in Level 13. His level, Level 12, he said, is the last level where you have to do any of the physical stuff, like assassinations. The higher up the group you go, the more you do the admin stuff, the checking, the emails, the organising.

Then he told me he wanted to leave Black Death. I didn't ask why. I didn't need to. He was running on a stream of chat and I was just lying there listening. 'It's not easy to get out,' he said. In order for him to leave, he would have to pay 1.5 million dollars and give all of his twenty properties to Black Death.

Then he turned to me and said he needed my help to

allow him to leave the group. It was a major task, he said. I hesitated. 'OK,' I said. 'What?'

And then he started to explain what I needed to do. It was, at first, very confusing. But he was so animated about this point, so anxious that I understood it correctly and that I would do exactly what he said. I will try to explain it now the best way I can.

In order for him to leave Black Death he wanted me to promote them. He wanted me to tell the media how Black Death worked and how their services could be provided. He wanted me to help the group 'recruit'. And there were bullet points he wanted me to say. I had to say that prices for assassination started at $75,000 and went up. I had to say that they use poison as their method of assassination, as no one investigates a heart attack. I also had to say that I had seen other girls. That particular point had come from CK. He said I had to explain that when the girls are kidnapped they will take a photo of her with the Black Death logo on a piece of paper, which also has the email details you can contact to bid for her.

Black Death don't currently operate in the UK, he said, but they wanted to expand. At the moment it is all eastern European audiences and he could use me to help get a UK audience. They wanted to get members from the UK to join. He saw me as a way to do that. He told me he had never been to the UK. He had heard of London, though, of course, and thought there would be opportunities there. He said, 'I know you live in London. Black Death know your address. They know where you and your mum live.'

I started to feel sick. I couldn't not agree to his terms. I couldn't argue or start saying I would never help him – where would that leave me? He could walk out and leave me here any moment to die. And then what? The mention of my mum was awful. I just needed to see her, to speak to her. It felt like a lifetime since I'd seen her. Time seemed to be going so slowly, it was agonising.

MD had found a notepad and we played quite a few games of hangman in it to pass the time. Does that sound weird? Now, I guess it does. Then, it was something to do, something to take my mind off where I was. He was very good at English. He knew lots of English words and it actually became quite competitive. We filled up the whole notebook with hangman games in the end. And he taught me how to play Battleships too. I had never played it before and it was something else to do.

★ ★ ★

It was some point later in the afternoon that we heard it. It was a low, rumbling sound at first and then it got louder and louder. There was no mistaking the noise, the chopper sound of the propellers as they whirred right above us – a helicopter! I sat up and looked up at the ceiling. I couldn't believe it! Had it come to rescue me? Was it trying to find me? MD was off the bed and pacing the room. He tried to look out through the shutters. The sound was so loud, it was like the helicopter was circling around and around over the roof of the house. MD didn't like it. He was paranoid and he started talking out loud – more to himself than me.

'The only way they would track you was if the Romanians had said something…if they had been bitter about being sacked,' he was muttering. 'But that would mean the death penalty for them. There's no way they know where you are.'

For those few precious moments my heart began to lift and I felt like this might be it – that the cavalry had come, that I would be rescued by the police, that Phil had sent in the army or the SAS to find me and bring me home.

It was hard not to build up my hopes. I stayed on the bed and I prayed. Why else would a helicopter be so close? What were they looking for?

The sound, that glorious sound, went on for about ten minutes. It was hovering. I thought it must be looking for me. If we were in such a desolate place, why would be it be hanging around for so long? It's got to be for me. Please be for me, I prayed. MD opened the shutters slightly and was fixed to the spot. He turned to me and said, 'If they come, you have to say I'm your boyfriend.' He made me say it out loud. I had to say, 'I will.' He seemed satisfied that I had agreed but, in my mind, I was determined to make some kind of covert signal to whoever was in the helicopter if it did land. But I wasn't ever going to try anything in front of the man I knew as MD.

If he was willing the helicopter to disappear, I was willing it equally hard to stay. But I didn't want to make it obvious. I didn't want him to see how excited I was about it. In the end, his will won out. The sound started to fade away, the noise receding into the distance, taking my hopes with it.

I was gutted. That was it. MD wouldn't settle for a long time after that. I think he was paranoid they would come back. He was on edge for the next hour or so before he started to convince himself, and me, that the helicopter wasn't a rescue party, it was just pure coincidence. He was so certain that there was no way they would find me unless the Romanians had said something, and he was pretty certain that wouldn't happen. Black Death wouldn't go easy on them. There was no way anyone knew where we were, he was telling me, no way. 'The helicopter was probably out looking for a hiker lost on the mountains,' he said. And that killed all sense of hope I had left.

★ ★ ★

That night, MD left his last email check of the day even later than usual. Maybe he was still paranoid about the helicopter, even though he had put on a good show of not giving it any more thought. But there was no more contact from Phil, no news at all. I just felt so alone. I felt abandoned and lost. The plate of food was still there, on the floor, untouched. A few flies had decided to land and see what they thought of it but I wasn't hungry. I didn't have an appetite. My water bottle had been replaced. He always gave me a new bottle, unopened, when I had finished the last one. And I always made sure it was sealed before I drank from it.

That night I lay thinking about everything that had happened. My bites started to itch but only because I deliberately scratched them. It gave me something to focus on. Getting to sleep that night was hard. I listened to him breathing in a deep sleep for a long time before I finally succumbed to slumber. The tears rolled down my face in a silent release and I just knew tomorrow would be no different. The only difference, I thought, was that it was a day nearer the auction starting. A day nearer to knowing my fate.

CHAPTER 7

Weak and weary

'He told me I was beautiful... he wanted to kiss me.'

Waking up on Friday morning, I felt different. I struggled to open my eyes and raise my head from the pillow. I hadn't eaten since Tuesday morning, when I had a quick breakfast in the hotel. I thought of that time as my 'old life' now, before this. So I hadn't eaten anything in my 'new life'. I wasn't hungry, due to stress, but I knew my body and I knew that I was suffering from lack of food as I was feeling so weak. I tried to put it out of my mind. The flies were all over the plate of food I had first been given on Tuesday and, however much I needed energy, I knew it would make me feel sick to try any of it. I would have to just cope. I would be OK. I closed my eyes again and let my mind drift back off. When I woke up, MD was looking at me intently. He had done the morning email check, he said, and there was nothing from Phil. I closed my eyes again. When would something happen? When would Phil help me?! I opened my eyes again and was taken a little bit by surprise when I saw MD still staring at me.

He then told me I was beautiful. I was taken aback. Up until this point there had been nothing but a professional air to him. He told me everything in black and white. Like what he was doing, what he did for Black Death, but it was all very business-like. There wasn't anything else but a kind of professionalism to him. But now things were changing; he was getting more personal. He had opened up a lot more to me since yesterday, when he told me he wanted to leave Black Death. He was talking about leaving a criminal organisation and all I wanted to concentrate on was being released.

He told me again that I was beautiful. He was trying to be flattering, to show affection, but I didn't know how to respond. This was a different person to the cold, abrupt person I'd met the first day. Now he was saying he wanted to kiss me. He wasn't physically trying to get near me, or forcing himself on me. It was like he wanted to just tell me.

'Thank you,' I said. Despite his flattery, I never felt, and I know some people don't understand this, that he was going to try anything or force himself on me.

This was unusual for him, he said. He didn't normally do this, get this involved with the kidnapped girls. It was unusual for him to be this involved, he persisted. If I had been a bitch he would have insisted the Romanians stay and watch me. But because I was OK, because I was being good, he said he was happy to stay with me. I wasn't screaming or shouting or behaving badly, he continued. I was good. Could he kiss me? he asked again. There was no way I was going to kiss this man. No way. But I never clearly said no. I never said never. I made sure that I didn't upset him. I didn't want to make him angry or cause any problems.

So my response, which has had a lot of debate in the media since then, was to tell him, maybe. Maybe in the future. What was I supposed to do? You tell me, if you were in my shoes, what would you have done? Would you have said no, never, the thought of kissing you repulses me? Or would you have played along, told him maybe…not now but one day? So that is what I did. I wasn't going to kiss him and I wasn't going to upset him and make him angry. So I did what I thought was the best thing to do, to say 'maybe'. I was leading him on. I was doing whatever I could to stay alive. I couldn't kiss him now, I said. I couldn't do anything while I was in this state. I just want to see my family. I couldn't think about anything else. 'Maybe when I'm free,' I said.

He seemed to be quite buoyed up by this and started saying that he would try everything – everything – to get me free, looking at me intently as he spoke. At this point, we were both waiting for Phil to make contact. He wanted to know that Phil was able to get the money. I just wanted to know that I would eventually be free. I knew the people I cared about would be missing me. It was such a horrible wait, such a horrible feeling. I just wanted to know what was happening, who was fighting on my side, and who cared about me?

I turned to MD. 'Once I'm free, once this is over,' I said,

'maybe we can see each other again.' They were just words – words to keep him happy and to give me a bit of power.

What was going through my mind when he said he wanted to kiss me? Apart from knowing that it was never going to happen, that I was never going to kiss him, I felt quite good that he felt like that about me. If he was developing feelings for me then it was a good sign. It would make it even more likely that he would help me, or so I thought. It was positive; he wouldn't want anything to happen to me. He cared about me and, although he didn't have the authority to actually release me, he told me his opinion meant a lot to the group. He had been there for five years and, at his level, people listened to him, he said. I believed him.

Acting the way he was now, a little less formal, warmer, surely meant that he saw me as more than just a job. He liked me, I thought. He must see me more as a human rather than a thing to sell. And you know what? All the time he wanted to kiss me, all the time his feelings grew meant that I was more than just a business transaction. If I could say the right things, I thought, I would be OK. He never physically acted on his feelings. He never pushed himself on me or tried to actually kiss me. It was just words. And I could use words too.

He had shown a softer side and I was going to do the same. He saw me as a woman – I needed him to see me as a daughter, a mother too. I talked about my mum. I told him how worried she would be about me. I talked about Ashton. I told him what a wonderful little boy he was, always smiling.

Ashton had his own bedroom, I said. I missed everything about him, being woken up in the night, the way he looked at me or cried for me when I left the room. He was starting to say words – baby gibberish, I call it. It was just a collection of sounds but it was like he thought he was telling me lots of interesting stuff.

It broke my heart talking about Ashton. Actually, physically, broke my heart. I could feel the pain in my chest. It was a feeling I will never forget and a feeling I never want to relive. I hadn't wanted to bring him into this situation. Saying his name out loud had seemed, until that point, all wrong. I had wanted to keep him in my head only; speaking his name meant I was bringing him into this horrible place, into this hell, and I wanted to protect him. I am his mother; it's my job to protect him.

★ ★ ★

I was allowed a shower again that morning and he gave me another pair of boxers and a T-shirt to put on. Again, they weren't brand new but they were washed and clean. Just the act of putting on fresh clothes each day was a blessing. The water from the shower helped my bites but standing up made me feel a little dizzy. It was another reminder from my body that I hadn't eaten anything. I was running on empty.

It wasn't that I had been doing anything but lying down – walking to the toilet and then lying down again wasn't exactly energetic. But my body still needed sustenance. Each day dragged on and on and those artificial lights…they gave no sense of time. The stream of constant brightness made my head ache and my eyes become hazy.

The rest of the day was spent listening to MD talk about Black Death. He had a new air of boastfulness about him now. He was bragging to me about Black Death and his methods of killing. It was chilling to hear and it felt like I had been plunged back into victim mode straight after briefly feeling semi-human. Now I felt frightened. This man was talking to me about murder and how he killed people. And not only that: he showed me the knives he carried.

'I am never unarmed,' he said. He took out a knife from his pocket, as if to show me he was serious. It was a flick-knife – one that flipped out when you pressed a button. He showed me another knife, a simple-looking sharp knife with a black handle.

'Go ahead, hold them,' he said to me. What should I do? There was no way I wanted to even see the knives, let alone hold them. I didn't say anything. 'Go on,' he pressed. 'Take them.'

So I did. They were lighter than I expected. I was sat on the bed holding them. I knew why he was showing them to me – he wanted some power back. He wanted to show me he had control. It was obvious he wanted to scare me. Don't try anything, was the unspoken message. I am armed and I will use them. Did I ever, even for a split second, feel like using them against him? This has been asked of me a lot. I can hand-on-my-heart confirm that I never thought of such a thing. Me, using a knife against a trained killer? I would be dead in seconds. So no, I never thought of using them.

He took them back and put them in his pocket and told me how he had used them recently. It wasn't on a job for Black Death, he said; it was two guys who'd annoyed him. He carried these knives for protection. He didn't want to use them, but sometimes people forced him to. He told me about when he was in Paris, and two Moroccan men went to clean his car without permission. They then demanded money from him, he said, for cleaning it. So he stabbed them. He said it so casually. It was a story to intimidate me and it worked. Then he told me how people staring at him triggers his anger. He would stare at them back, he said, until they were forced to turn away.

'Would you like to see the photos?' he asked. I felt my heart actually stop for a moment. My brain was trying to understand what he said. Photos of the men he'd stabbed? My mouth went dry but I was able to ask, 'What photos?'

And he told me. 'Photos of you,' he said.

I couldn't breathe. I actually felt the breath go out of my body and I couldn't physically make myself take any more in. I was in shock. Whether he was oblivious to what I was thinking, or whether this was part of his plan of complete control, I don't know. But he kept on talking.

'They have to take pictures of the girls to prove they have captured them, and you were no different,' he said. 'There are a lot of fake Black Death websites out there. We need to prove we are the real thing, that we have the proof. We can't just put out a link to the girls' social media pages, what would that prove?'

It was so surreal, so abstract listening to him explain this.

He couldn't possibly be talking about girls, young girls, me…could he?

'The Romanians have a fifteen-minute time slot from when they actually kidnap the girl to loading her in the car,' he was explaining. 'And in that fifteen minutes they have to strip the girls to search for a tracker. That's why you were stripped,' he said. 'Some models always have them; it is very common. And long hair is a usual place to hide them.'

I was starting to piece it together. I had never questioned why I found myself in the boot of the car with only my pink bodysuit on. Weirdly, at the time it was a blessing, as I was so hot in the car, but I had not started to process why my clothes had been taken until now. Maybe I didn't want to. Maybe I didn't even want my mind to go down that route of what might have happened to me once the syringe went in. I let him carry on talking. I was hanging on his every word.

Then he turned to me. 'I can give you a tracker when you are released, then I will always be able to find you.' It was a statement and I wasn't going to agree or disagree. He carried on. 'They took a picture of you when you were drugged,' he said. 'Do you want to see it?'

For the first time since he'd started talking about the photos and the process of being kidnapped I knew exactly how I felt. 'Yes,' I said, without hesitation. This was a blank in my life – a time when I had no idea what had happened to me. Yes, I wanted to see my photo.

He didn't seem surprised. I would have to wait, he said, until he did his lunchtime email check. He would have to download the advert from the deep web and put it on his laptop. So I had to wait. He told me that CK was still waiting to hear from Phil, but if Phil was able to get some money from one of the people whose names I had given him, he was sure CK would be happy for me to pay the remaining balance on my release. There would be strict terms and conditions, he said, but that might be a possibility. Yes, yes! I thought. I could do that, I said. I could pay it back. There was no way I would really be able to do this, there was no way I could get that sort of money, but I didn't care. It was a way out of this nightmare. It was a glimmer of hope.

He continued to talk about Black Death. He told me he stored money he had earned in the form of gold. He told me he wanted to build houses in Scotland that were nuclear bomb-proof. He told me how the property we were in was special to him because of the cows he owned. The cows would be sold to a farmer once he gave up the house. When he buys a new property, people from Black Death come in and paint it. Well, the ones working at lower levels do. He doesn't bother to keep any of the furniture. 'It's all cheap,' he said. 'None of it is important.'

He got up suddenly then and went out of the room. This was it, I thought. When he comes back I will see it. It felt like hours but was probably only twenty minutes at most. There had been no emails from Phil. Nothing had come through. He was really shocked; he couldn't believe Phil didn't care. When he came back, he was carrying a laptop and he brought it over to the bed. He sat up on the bed and put it on his lap. I didn't have to wait for him to start it up or find the photo – it was right there in front of me on the screen. It was me. I was in an advert. I saw everything.

'I saw this,' he said. 'This was how I knew you were being held. This was why I drove from Rome to here. I could see you were up for auction.'

I forced myself to stare at the screen and look at myself. It was me but it wasn't me. If I couldn't remember it happening, could it actually be true? But there I was, staring right back out of the screen at me. Although I wasn't staring out at anyone, I looked like I was…well, dead. That was my first thought. There was no life in that picture, there was no life in my eyes. I was unconscious, I knew, from the drugs. I studied the photo intently. So this was my online auction picture. This was the photo they had to use to prove it was a real sale and that I was in their hands, ready to be sold to the highest bidder. There was a link to my Instagram account, I saw then. Just at the bottom. 'So buyers know what you look like at other times,' said MD. 'So they can see more photos of you.'

There was a big part of me that wanted to look away, that didn't want to see the advert any more, but it felt strange. It didn't feel like I was looking at me. I had no idea what they had done to me after that needle went in my arm, but I was now being shown what had happened. They had undone my jeans, untied my trainers, pulled off my jacket and 'positioned' me on the floor for the world to see. Not the world I lived in, but a dark, evil world that wanted to buy me.

Did it make me angry? Angry is probably the wrong word. It was all so professional on their side. It wasn't like

I didn't feel anger they'd done this, but I was shocked that it appeared so expertly done, so practised. The structure of what they did – it was so authoritative. How could I ever doubt what he was saying when he was showing me all this stuff?

I was lying next to him on the bed and I made myself look at the writing underneath my picture. It said I was being held in Germany. It gave my measurements. It said my age, nineteen. I realised of course that that was why they were so keen to have my exact measurements for the motorbike leathers photo shoot. They had to be precise, not for me to fit into custom-made clothes, but for when I went up for sale.

So I was in Germany? OK, at least it gave me a sense of location. Nineteen... I was nineteen years old when I went to Paris for the original shoot, the one where they had first planned to take me. They didn't know I'd had a birthday since, that I was now twenty.

All this text was specific to me and then I saw underneath: 'Terms and Conditions'. I started reading it. It talked about delivery, how they capture to meet specific needs. Then MD shut the laptop. I sat back, trying to erase the photo from my mind. It was just a picture, I told myself. I am OK.

'What do you remember?' he asked me. 'How did they take you?'

I wasn't sure why he wanted to know all of this but he was persistent. 'Did they inject you?'

'Yes,' I replied.

'Good,' he said. 'Sometimes they knock a girl unconscious

by beating them. It's not good for the photos necessarily but it gets the job done. As long as they are unconscious they can be prepped for the advert. 'I know what drug they would have used,' he said.

'What?!' I was desperate to know. At first he didn't tell me but I insisted. I needed to know what was in me.

'Ketamine,' he said. And he gave me a specific dosage of what they used. Then he asked, 'Did they rape you?'

'No,' I said. 'No.' I have to tell you, I'm sure I would have known if something like that had happened. It's what helped me to answer so determinedly 'No'. I was saying it again as if to reassure myself.

'Good. It would be the death penalty for them if they had,' he said.

He put the laptop on the floor and took out an ID card from his pocket. It was a Polish card, an identification card or something like that. I saw the name on it: Daniel somebody. There was a photo, too, and it looked like him but it had obviously been doctored in some way, although I couldn't tell you exactly what was different. He told me he photoshops the photos slightly, and that he used fake ID cards for hiring out places, studios, houses, to keep the girls in. Or for storing drugs. Then he would just snap the card and apply for a new one for the next job.

This one, he said, was just one of thousands he had used over the years. He told me he was going outside to cut up the card and burn it. I heard him go downstairs and slam the front door. He must be doing what he said he was doing, I thought.

Later that evening – much, much later, after he had done his nightly email check around midnight – he came in with some chocolate. Small squares of milk chocolate that had been left on top of their wrapper and on a plate. That was suspicious. Why not give it to me still in the wrapper? Why did he have to open it and break it up? But I was so hungry and felt so weak I just needed something. OK, so it might be poisoned, but that was a chance I had to take. I had to eat something. So I did, and it felt good. I felt so much better in myself. I thought I might eat it all in one go. I was so hungry, but I suppose there was still a bit of suspicion left in me so I ate it slowly. I'm not normally a fan of chocolate but I felt so weak and this helped.

I closed my eyes that night and cried again. I was one day closer to knowing what was going to happen to me. Was that my last meal? A few measly squares of chocolate? I felt a sense of hope that day – MD wanted to help me – but with no word from Phil, no idea what was happening in England, I had no sense of whether my hope was futile. Were these my last days alive? I had done everything I should have done, I thought. I was engaging in conversations, and I wasn't showing any anger towards him. I should have been screaming and shouting at him but I wasn't. I could have easily been screaming and shouting. Do I wish I had fought back? Shouted and screamed until I was blue in the face at the man holding me captive? No, I might not be here today if I'd done anything different.

I am the only one who knows how I should have acted. And I have survived. Talk to me when you've been in that situation. Tell me then what you did, how you reacted. I did what I did and I'm alive because of it.

CHAPTER 8

Facing my fate

'I had no strength and now I had no hope.'

I woke up in the morning with a sense of dread. There was one more day, just one, until I knew my fate. My auction would begin and I would be sold into a life of rape and torture and murder. I wouldn't see my son or mum again. I wouldn't see my friends again. My life wouldn't be worth living. And yet, I still had some hope. I was clinging on to the hope that Black Death would be happy to release me if I agreed to pay the money. If Phil could raise some of the money and I agreed to pay the rest. MD was certain that CK would be happy with that. It was a mistake that I had been taken. MD was trying all he could to help me and this was an option. It was such a small flicker of hope, but it was hope. I had absolutely no idea how I would ever pay back such a large amount of money but I didn't care – I would be free. I would do or say anything to make it happen.

MD came into the room that morning with news. He had done his email checks and Phil had made contact. Phil had told him he was able to get £20,000 from one of the names I had given him. I held my breath. This was it. But before I could let that sink in, he continued. CK thought they might be able to get more money from Phil, he said. So Black Death wanted to wait a few more days to see if they could get more money. I would have to stay here for longer while they tried to get more money in exchange for my life.

I broke down. This was the first time I had cried in front of him. My whole body, which had been so tense while listening to MD talk, just collapsed. I had no strength and now I had no hope. This couldn't be happening. The thought of staying here a day longer, an hour longer, a minute longer, was too much to bear. I sobbed with my whole body, with my heart and soul, and I didn't care.

'What about the deal that I would pay back the money on my release?' I sobbed. I thought we were on the right track. I was trying to convince him that Phil wouldn't be able to raise any more. £20,000 would be as much as he could get. 'He won't be able to help!' I screamed at him. 'Phil is just playing for time. There is no more money.'

I honestly thought, when MD told me about the possibility of paying the money back on my release, we were on the right track. And now Phil had ruined everything.

'Please believe me,' I sobbed. 'Phil won't be able to get any more money.'

MD watched me and spoke. 'OK, I will tell CK what you have told me.' And he left the room. He's gone to email CK, I thought. Please let CK believe him, please let them believe there is no more money.

I knew MD wasn't happy with Phil. He was angry that he had responded to one of his emails to CK instead of directly to him. The email MD had sent to Phil asking for three people who might be able to raise money was done behind CK's back, without Black Death knowing. Now Phil had responded to that email, saying he could get £20,000 from one of the names, but he had sent that to CK. CK didn't know anything about MD's email about getting three names. And now MD was panicking. He was stressing out as Phil shouldn't have sent that email to Black Death, only back to MD.

'If CK finds out I've been making contact with Phil behind Black Death's back…'

There was no doubting the fear in MD's voice. Had he done something he would be punished for?

I was devastated. I was inconsolable. I waited for him to come back. I lay on the bed and closed my eyes. I don't know how long he was gone but the moment I heard the beads rattle in the door frame my eyes flew open.

CK was furious with Phil, who hadn't been using the correct procedure to contact Black Death. I didn't understand what he was talking about but I sat and waited to hear what this meant for me. Phil should have been going through the deep web, there was a set pattern to follow, a code for someone to operate on the deep web, but he wasn't, and CK wasn't happy. 'He is pissed off,' said MD. 'I think he believes me that he won't get any more money from Phil.'

It was something but it was also nothing. I started to cry again. I wasn't any closer to knowing what was going to happen to me – whether I would have to stay there longer to wait for them to get more money, for an auction for my life. I'm not sure if in that moment he felt so sorry for me and that he wanted to do something to cheer me up, or if he was always going to tell me what he was about to reveal. But he came over and sat on the bed next to me.

'I have lied to you, Chloe,' he said. 'We are still in Italy.'

I didn't know what to say or what to think. I was still in Italy. OK, I was trying to process this. What did it mean for me? It was a comfort. I did feel a sense of…relief, I guess, but I'm not sure why. It wasn't like I knew where I was. I had never been to Italy before coming to Milan. But then my mind clicked into gear.

'The advert…my picture…it said I was being held in Germany,' I said. Quick as a flash, no sense of hesitation, he replied. Apparently the Romanians were meant to take me to Germany but they came here instead. One of them had to leave for another job halfway through, which explained why there was only one masked man and the driver instead of two. He told me the driver was the same nationality as him but he wouldn't tell me what that was.

'I am doing everything I can to help you, Chloe,' he said. 'But I can't release you unofficially. I would be put to death.'

He was scared. I could see it in his eyes and hear it in

his voice. And that's what got me. He was an assassin, a trained killer, and he was scared of Black Death. What hope did I have? An organisation that could strike fear into one of its high-level assassins wasn't going to think twice about killing me. I had been told I was being watched, that Black Death would find me even if I ran, and that more members were operating in the area. I could see the hold they had over MD. I would do exactly as I was told. I would do everything I could to be released. Escaping wasn't an option. They would catch me and kill me. I was sure of it.

'CK doesn't believe he will get any more money from Phil,' he said again. 'If you agree to pay the remaining money, you will be released. CK is happy with that arrangement but we have to wait for the official release letter to come through. Everything has to be official,' he said. There was no way I could afford to pay the money but there was no way I wasn't going to agree to this. Now I just had to wait for the email checks and see if CK had really decided that I could be released.

★ ★ ★

I was so upset that day, it seemed that everything was going wrong one minute and then I had such hope the next. I could be released, but would I be released? MD saw that I was still upset. He didn't try to physically comfort me. Instead, he used words to heal me. He told me he had lied to me before; we weren't as remote as he had first said. He told me he'd lied to save my life. He thought that if he had said we weren't as isolated as we were, I might try to escape. And with Black Death watching my every move, it would be instant death. So he lied to protect me, he said. He was trying to keep me alive but also keep himself alive. This made sense in my mind. And I believed him. If Black Death were watching my every move there was no way I was going to try to escape and get killed.

'There is a village,' he said. 'I will take you there tomorrow. You will need trainers when you are released. I will need to take you to the consulate on Monday but you will have to walk some of the way there, as I can't be seen. We will go tomorrow to get trainers.'

My head was spinning. I was hearing the words but I couldn't get them to make any sense. Monday? The consulate? I wasn't sure what was going on. MD wasn't making sense and yet it sounded like he had everything planned.

'You will be officially released, don't worry,' he continued. He told me that CK would arrange it all; a letter would come through. We just had to wait until that happened. Then I would have to pay the money when I was released.

Going to a village? A village, tomorrow? I would see daylight! I would be outside, fresh air... I would see people... It was too much to take in. This was going to be amazing. I wanted to be excited. I hadn't seen daylight for so long, just artificial light. Would I really be able to see the sun? I hadn't stretched my legs for so long. I had walked from the bathroom to the bed and back again, but that was it. Now I would be able to go out and feel the sun on my face, and breathe in the fresh air. God, I was so giddy with the thought of it.

Although, what if he changed his mind? I was still unable to relax. Would MD have to get permission from CK to take me out of the house? It seemed like MD was doing all he could to help me. 'I make you no promises,' he had said. 'If it was up to me, it would be fine, but it's not up to me.'

You see, this is where I find it difficult to explain to people, to the police, to the media, about my relationship with MD. To me, he was always trying to help me. He was the one who was acting like he was rescuing me from Black Death. I get a lot of people asking me to explain why I did what I was told, and why I didn't get cross with him. 'But he was your kidnapper. He was keeping you hostage,' they say.

But in my mind, in that situation, he was the one who had come in and intervened. And he was the one who was so incensed about the young mother rule, he was trying everything he could to get Black Death to release me. So that's why I didn't try to attack him, or escape, or fight him… to me, in my eyes, he was my only hope.

The media seems to think I should have behaved differently. That I should have realised he was one of the masked men. But I never thought that at the time. It was something I registered only weeks later. Then, in that situation, when he started talking about finding ways to help me, and talking about the consulate, he was someone who wanted to help me. He was the one answering my questions. He was the one keeping me alive.

The rest of the day was spent in a daze of questions, and

my mind started filling with hope. He brought up a plate of food from downstairs and was eating it on the bed next to me. It looked like ham and gherkins. He didn't offer me any but I couldn't take my eyes off the plate and he caught me staring. He offered me some. He was eating it, so it was safe. It couldn't have been poisoned. I needed my strength if I was to walk tomorrow, if I was to do anything tomorrow that wasn't just lying down. I needed to be strong. I needed to be focused.

'Do you want some?' he asked. He had stopped eating and was asking me if I wanted to share his food. I did. I had an appetite all of a sudden. I was beginning to feel less stressed, and I was building up hope for release on Monday. It tasted awful. I would never eat this sort of thing at home, but I was so hungry. And it helped. It would keep up my strength. He brought me a can of Red Bull too. Apparently the Romanian had left it, he said, and would I like it? It was the weirdest feeling, drinking that fizzy liquid. Red Bull was my favourite drink, and when I took that first sip, I had such an immense feeling of homesickness. This was a taste that reminded me of home. I closed my eyes and I could picture myself on my sofa, in my front room. It was such a normal taste and yet this wasn't normal.

I felt a bit happier that night. MD had spent the afternoon explaining how the letter from Black Death ordering my release would work. He explained what it meant. I couldn't just say goodbye and that would be it. It had to be official, he said, and that meant I would be on a list. Once someone is released, he said, which is extremely rare, Black Death can't touch them again. You get put on a list that will protect you from harm against the group for ever.

'How does that feel?' he asked. 'How does it feel to be protected against the biggest criminal organisation in the world?'

I know he wanted me to feel some sort of excitement, or gratitude, but I didn't know what to think. I must admit, I was worried that even if I did ever get out of there, what was to stop me being captured again? Who was to say I might not ever be kidnapped again? But he was trying to show me that this wouldn't happen. My name being on this list would protect me. There are so few names on the list, he said. Only a handful of people, and you will be among them. It was like he was making it out to be such an accolade, such an award.

'There are probably only five girls on the list,' he said, and went on to explain: they were on it because they were captured and then released. They might have been pregnant or their government or parents bought them out of the auction. Those people are on the list but it doesn't happen very often. There were strict rules for the release policy.

I knew I would have to pay back the money, and that was what scared me the most – how on earth I would manage that. But he had an answer for that too. I would do lots of promoting of Black Death in the media, he said. People would want to know my story. I would be paid for interviews and that is how I could get the money. He had it all worked out. But there would be strict rules. He knew I had to obey release conditions.

He told me stories that evening about how other people had tried to do their own thing and go against the rules. He told me there was an MP in London whose family were raped and tortured in front of him before he was killed. And then he said sometimes Black Death would bribe the police. If the police had one of their agents in prison, and they had kidnapped a girl, sometimes they would try to bribe the police to release their agent in exchange for a girl. He wasn't saying this to scare me, he was just talking casually. Whatever he told me, I now had some hope. I didn't want to have it but it was there, like a little beacon in my brain, and if I clung on to it then maybe everything would be OK.

We were now waiting for an email from CK and Black Death confirming my release agreement. He went out that night to do his usual checks. If waiting for news from Phil was worrying, this felt a hundred times worse. I was in touching distance of leaving this place, of being able to go, and yet what if they changed their minds? What if they decided I should just be put up for auction instead? I was so tense. I was sitting on the edge of the bed waiting for him to come back into the room and tell me. Had something gone wrong? Was it all OK? My fate was in other people's hands, and even though I was now being told there was an end, I could see a way out, and Black Death seemed willing to release me, I didn't want to believe it until I was out of the house. And, oh my God, the thought of seeing sunlight, of having fresh air, was almost too much to bear. I would do everything he said. I would continue to do everything I was told, and I would be OK.

Tomorrow wasn't going to be the auction for my life; tomorrow would be a day when I could remember I was a human being. I closed my eyes and tried to get some sleep.

CHAPTER 9

Fresh air and fresh fruit

'I couldn't open my eyes properly at first…
it was so bright.'

We woke up really early Sunday morning. The clock said 7am. It was excitement on my part, I know. I was so keen to actually get out. He would always wake up really early and put the light on, so I was used to waking up early, even though all I wanted to do was sleep and make the day seem less long. He put on the little heater in the room, which he did every morning, as it was quite chilly. I just wanted to get up and go. But he had to do something first.

He had an erection. It was pretty obvious. He was moaning about it, how he was in pain because of it, he said. He couldn't walk properly. He was bent over, saying he would have to do something about it. It was a build-up from the past couple of days, he said. He told me to go and have a shower. That he had to sort himself out. So I did. I didn't question anything. I made sure I took a long time in the shower. I washed my hair and took ages drying it in the bathroom. I didn't want to go back out into the bedroom for a long time afterwards. He didn't say anything, and didn't mention it afterwards. It was done. I was concentrating on getting out of the house. I looked at the clock: it was 9am. Time to go.

I walked down the concrete stairs in a bit of a daze and through the kitchen that I hadn't stepped foot in for four days. I hadn't stepped foot anywhere except the bedroom and bathroom and now I was going to be outside. Seeing daylight for the first time was just…it was crazy. I can't describe the feeling. I couldn't open my eyes properly at first, it was so bright. There was so much brightness everywhere, I had to stand by the front door and let my eyes adjust. I was shocked by the beautiful view in front of me. The mountain scenery…it was so unexpected.

Now I had to get my legs working. It was like I was learning to walk again, they felt so shaky. I had had no exercise in just a few days but it was like my muscles had completely forgotten what to do.

MD wasn't hanging around; he wasn't waiting for me and I didn't want to be left out there alone, so I willed them to work… one foot in front of the other, as I made my way slowly down the path from the house.

The outside walls were white, I noticed, and it looked a lot better on the outside than it did on the inside. I wanted to stop and get my bearings, to see if there were other people around, or other houses, but MD told me to come on. We had to go down a little hill to the car and I was walking so slowly. But I couldn't have moved any faster if I'd tried!

I was wearing the blue tracksuit he'd given me. It had the word 'Polska' or something on the back. He told me it wasn't his; it was left at the house. I had a white T-shirt under it, and a pair of sliders with a prickly sole that were too big for me. They were so uncomfortable and weren't helping with my lack of walking ability. As well as being bright, the sun shone fiercely and it felt so hot. Or maybe I had just forgotten what the sun felt like on my face, but I felt like I was burning up. It wasn't even midday sun, just a normal summer's morning.

I paused on the hill and looked around. There were massive mountains right in front of me and really tall trees everywhere. There were lots of ruins scattered around too; not houses that had been left derelict, but actual stone ruins. Buildings that had been long abandoned. The hill we were walking down was steep and the path was made up of stepping stones. It was hard to negotiate, and MD was walking down quite quickly while I was proceeding really slowly. I didn't want to fall or injure myself but I didn't want him to think I was being deliberately slow or difficult. I looked up, and that was when I saw the car. The blue car. It was parked just a few feet in front of us, at the bottom of the hill. This was the car I had been bundled into at the start of my ordeal – the car that had transported me here, held me captive in its boot and then released me to my new prison.

There were a few questions in my mind as I approached the car. I was replaying a conversation I'd had with MD the previous night. He told me that this was the car that had transported me here but now I was thinking, How would he know that? How would he know what car I'd travelled in? He told me he had come from Rome, so why would he have this car? It didn't make sense to me but I didn't say anything. At the time, when he said we would be going to the village in the car I was held in the boot of, I said to him, 'The silver car?' I remember I used those exact words: 'The silver car'. When I was lying in the boot and it was opened, I could make out that part of the side of the car was silver. He was adamant it was blue, though.

I thought I was getting confused. Perhaps it was the bright, sudden sunlight. I didn't know. He opened the passenger door for me and I sat down. I had asked him the previous day if I would be able to travel in the front and he said yes. He was going to blindfold me, he said, but in the end, this morning, we had walked down as equals. It showed the trust we had built over the past few days. He had changed his mind and I wasn't going to remind him what he'd said the night before.

It felt so normal but so surreal getting into a car. I was another step closer to being released and I was praying our trip would go well and MD would stick to his word. He still hadn't had any official release documents through from CK, but he said they would come. He didn't seem worried. He started the car and, as the road was quite narrow, he had to turn round and he took his time reversing and manoeuvring.

There were lots of narrow, windy roads to negotiate in order to get to the bottom of the mountain. He said it took seven minutes to get to the bottom of the mountain but I'm not sure why he told me that. He was driving fast, and he took all the corners really sharply. I couldn't quite understand why we were going so fast but then I looked out of the window and I saw an old man or woman, I couldn't tell which, gardening. He or she was bent over on their knees on the grass near one of the ruins. I stared. I couldn't help myself. I willed this person, who I'd decided was female, to look up and see me but they didn't. She didn't seem to care about the car passing her so quickly. Even if she had looked up, I don't suppose, at the speed we were going, that she would have seen me.

When we reached the bottom of the mountain, the road opened up a little more and became wider. It was more like a normal road now but there were still no cars. There were lots of fields either side, though, and we did pass a few cars as we travelled along but, by then, the roads were like normal and we weren't close enough or slow enough to see anyone inside. I tried to focus, tried to make sense of where we were. I looked for signs, for names of places, but there were hardly any. I remember seeing one sign that had the word VIU on it. Was that the name of where we were? Where we were headed? It meant nothing to me and I felt pretty useless at that point. What was the point of trying to look out for signs if I didn't know what they meant?

★ ★ ★

We had probably been in the car about fifteen or twenty minutes when the roads narrowed into one-track lanes as we approached a small village. MD parked in a little car park. I reached out for the handle to let myself out, and MD let out a little noise. 'Uh uh,' he said. I was to sit still until I was let out. He came round the front of the car and opened my door for me. I stood by the side of the car, taking in my surroundings.

It felt so good to be out of that house; it felt normal. It was everything I had been missing, the normality of it all. You take it for granted – the sunshine, the fresh air, the ordinariness of going to a village. It was so, so nice. And I saw people going about their normal lives. I looked over to the other side of the road and saw a couple walking down the street. Just walking together. They weren't doing anything out of the ordinary, just strolling along in the sunshine. I thought to myself, they are so lucky. They have a normal life. They don't know how lucky they are. And then I heard a dog bark and I turned round and saw a man walking his dog. My heart ached so much. I missed walking my dog. I missed my normal routine of walking my excitable, loyal beagle every morning and watching her chase after everything and anything she could.

I wanted to yell. I wanted to scream and shout, and in my head I was. In my head I was bellowing, 'It's not fair! You're normal! I want to be normal!' But of course, I couldn't do anything. I didn't know who was watching. MD had told me the agents of Black Death were always around. They were everywhere, and you would never know if you were being watched. I had to be so careful – I was so scared that someone was watching me.

We walked down a little street. He reached for my hand and I held it. I felt I had to. Instinctively I put my other hand across my chest. I knew he was the one protecting me from other Black Death members who might be watching and I didn't want to refuse to hold his hand and upset him. Then I would have no one, I thought. There was no pavement, so we had to stay close to the side, right by the edge of the road.

We then went to a shoe shop, a mountain-hiking kind of place. Before he opened the door, MD turned to me and told me he was going to pretend he didn't speak Italian. I have no idea why. He just said it. But he can speak five languages, or at least that's what he told me previously; why would he want to pretend he couldn't speak Italian?

I didn't question it. I just nodded. We went through the door and I pointed to the first pair of trainers I saw. He took them to the woman by the counter, the shopkeeper. She spoke to him in Italian. He looked round at me and asked me my shoe size. 'Five,' I said. But she only had size six. He went over to the woman to pay for them. She was about sixty years old, I would guess. She spoke in Italian and he answered in English. She didn't say anything to me, why would she? I just sat in the corner. I put my shoes on. I was doing as I was told. He paid forty-something euros for them, I think. We were probably in the shop a few minutes, no more than that. We went in the shop, he shoved a pair of trainers at me, I put them on and he bought them. That was that.

And yet, such a fuss has been made over that event.

I had lied. I had deliberately lied to the police. I had

misled them and had spent the day shoe shopping with MD, laughing and joking and having fun. This is what the papers had reported. This is what I have had to defend myself about in the British media. After so many hours of talking about my ordeal, when I was asked about the tracksuit and trainers, I don't actually recall what I said. When I was questioned specifically about the trainers I answered everything fully and to the satisfaction of the prosecutor. When I was questioned about this on *Good Morning Britain*, I felt like I was defending myself against weeks of accusations that this whole kidnapping was faked. It was a strong line of questioning and I had no qualms in answering it.

The newspapers, the tabloids, they all seem to think I enjoyed an afternoon shopping for shoes. 'Model's shoe shopping trip', I think the *Sun* described it as. Yet for me, it was another part of being controlled. I had no control over what we did or where we went. I was so petrified of doing something wrong, of upsetting MD, of not doing as I was told. This might sound strange but the whole time we were out of the house felt like an out-of-body experience to me.

I wasn't myself; I didn't feel I had any say in what was happening or what we did. I wasn't me, if that makes sense. I was being operated. I was under a spell; being hypnotised, in a sense. I am sorry, but I can't really explain it – it was me but it wasn't me. I was like a machine being controlled. We left the shop and I followed MD, who was carrying the bag with his sliders in it. We then had to walk back up the windy road again, back to the car. There was a grocery store next to the car park, a little fruit shop. It was one of those stores with some stands outside displaying lots of fruit.

'Shall we get some fruit?' he suggested. I nodded. I love fruit and I was so happy when he said that. The shop was so tiny I didn't think we would both fit in, but he insisted I follow him in to pay. He picked up peaches, plums, kiwi fruit, then paid the shopkeeper and that was it. Back to the car.

There was such a big part of me that loved being outside but I couldn't say I was free. I couldn't say I wanted to stay out there longer. MD was always saying there were lots of Black Death agents nearby. So I liked being outside but I was scared of other people. I couldn't tell who was an agent. They could be anyone, anyone walking past, and I wouldn't know. He put such fear in me. I was scared all the time. I was being controlled by him and I just wanted to get back to the house at that point.

So when people ask me, 'Why didn't you run?' 'Why didn't you try to escape?' 'Why didn't you raise the alarm, send out a message, scream for help?' There is my answer. I was under the evil spell that Black Death were watching my every move. That even if I escaped, even if I somehow got free of MD, then what? I wasn't safe. I would be tracked down and killed, that is what he said. MD was trying to help get me released. He was my best bet for survival. I had to do what he said.

Getting back to the house, where it was just him and me, it felt safe. No one else could get to me. I was so close to getting the release letter – MD said it would come today, it had to come today – that I didn't want to mess anything up. I was so close. I was nearly there. If I made one wrong move, or if someone interfered, it would all be messed up. I had waited all this time. I was only one day away. And I was desperate for it to go OK.

There was only one way back to the house and we travelled in silence. We drove back up the mountain and parked the car in the same spot. I waited for him to open the door for me and let me out, and then there was the walk back up the hill to the house. If I thought walking downhill was bad, walking back up was even worse. My legs kept cramping and seizing up and I had to keep stopping. It was like my legs had gone to sleep. The trainers were a lot easier to walk in than the sliders, but because they were one size too big they weren't ideal to help me navigate the path.

I looked up at the house as we approached it. It looked like a normal, rural, white house. Nothing strange from the outside, but it was my prison. I was trying to picture where the bedroom was – was I being kept in the back or the front of the house? In the bedroom there were two big wooden shutters and I realised when I saw them from outside that the bedroom was at the front of the house. I had worked out my bearings. I was trying to do all I could to make myself feel a bit more in control. The house looked bigger than I'd thought, and it wasn't until we were right near the front of it that I noticed a little outbuilding, a smaller building just off to the right of the house that was part of it without being actually attached to it. As we were walking past, MD stopped and pointed over to the small building. And he said,

Left: Two-year-old me

Above: On holiday when I was four years old

Left: With Wolfy the Alsatian. I have always loved dogs

Left: When I was six years old

Above: On holiday when I was eight.
The beach was my favourite place

Left: Four years old

Left: My first shoot after what happened in Italy

Above: Me and my five-year-old beagle, Nylah

Left: Visiting Blausee in Bern, Switzerland

Above: Boot of the car in which I was transported after being drugged and kidnapped

Right: Lukasz Herba, as photographed by police after his arrest

Above: The farmhouse near Turin where I was held for six days in July 2017

Left: Black Death Group leaflet found by police at bogus photography studio in Milan from where I was kidnapped

BLACK DEATH GROUP

BLACKDEATHGROUP@SAFE-MAIL.NET
BLACKDEATHGROUP@BITMESSAGE.CH
BLACKDEATHGROUP@TORBOX3UIOT6IWCHZ.ONION
BLACKDEATHGROUP@TUTANOTA.COM
BLACKDEATHGROUP@PROTONMAIL.COM

Right: Lukasz Herba in
the Milan courtroom
during his trial

Left: During the trial, the
photo of me drugged and
unconscious was shown
to the court

Above: Being inter-
viewed by Eammon
Holmes and Ruth
Langsford on *This
Morning*, 14 August 2017

© *Ken McKay/Rex/Shutterstock*

Right: Me, photographed
for the *Sun* newspaper
after the verdict

© *Dan Charity – the* Sun

as if he was casually telling me the time of day, 'That's where the girls normally stay.'

I stopped dead in my tracks and looked at the building, which was little more than a hut. There was an odd little door at the front and no windows.

'They're chained to a big beam that sits high up near the ceiling' he said. 'They are chained to the beam with their arms above their heads so they can literally just touch the ground on their tiptoes.' I wanted to get past that place as soon as I could but MD was blocking the path and not moving. 'Do you want to see?' he asked.

Did I want to see?! No, no, no, I screamed in my head. But instead of speaking I just shook my head. I didn't want to. I was so scared. It was so spooky walking past that building. I didn't want to imagine what happened in there. It was terrifying... I couldn't imagine what it must have been like to stand there, with your arms chained above you. I think he was telling me this to make me feel grateful that I had a bed and stuff to sleep on. He was always bragging about that. If I was a bitch about the situation, I would still be chained up, he had said to me so many times. If the Romanians had me, if he let them be in charge of me, they wouldn't have even let me go to the toilet. He was trying to make me feel grateful and respect him. And thankful that I wasn't one of the girls in that building. I hurried past it – you had to go right past it to get back through the little front garden and to the front door.

We went back into the house. I stood in the kitchen for a moment. A sense of relief and of dread hit me at exactly the same time. I didn't want to be back here but it wasn't going to be for long; one more night, I told myself. At least I wasn't in that building, I thought to myself. Those poor girls… I mustn't think of them, but it was hard not to. I was doing the right things. I was doing what I needed to do to survive. I knew I wouldn't be allowed to stay in the kitchen or roam freely in the house, so I started moving towards the stairs, but something caught my attention out of the corner of my eye. It looked like a child's toy…a plastic toy. Why would there be a kid's toy there? He didn't rent it out, he'd said. I couldn't work out why or what that was doing there, so I put it out of my mind as I climbed back up the stairs.

MD stayed in the kitchen. He would prepare the fruit, he said. I waited on the bed. I needed to rest my legs; how pathetic is that? After that short walk they felt completely drained. It took ages for MD to come up. I waited for him, lying on the bed and, although my body was grateful for the rest, it felt horrible going back into that airless room after escaping it for a few short hours. I felt like I was being teased. I'd had a taste of fresh air, a taste of daylight, and now I was back in that room. It felt like I had never gone out. It was horrible. It seemed to take ages but he eventually came up with the fruit. It had been cut up into small pieces and arranged very decoratively on the plate. He had obviously spent a long time doing it. He was eating it as he came in. I don't know why he had gone to so much effort in cutting it all up but he had and as I saw him eating it I knew it was safe to eat. It tasted so good. So, so good.

Mid-mouthful he suddenly got up from the bed and opened the balcony windows. The shutters were open and there was such a wonderful breeze coming through. I jumped off the bed and went to look. He didn't say anything and I took that to mean I was allowed to go out on the balcony. I took a step forward and the view took my breath away. It was so beautiful. He wasn't worried about me being outside and seeing where we were. We were going tomorrow and it didn't matter, he said.

He came out on to the balcony with me and I noticed lots of those little lizards skittering around. I watched them stay as still as statues and then shoot so fast across the floor and off into the bushes. They were funny to watch and it seemed so strange to me that I was happy. I felt happy watching them. I felt happy at the fresh air. I was happy at the thought of tomorrow.

★ ★ ★

He would check his emails soon, he said. He was waiting for the letter from Black Death, the official release letter. He knew what it was going to say. 'But you have to read it and understand,' he said. Basically it would give the reason for my release and what I had to do to settle the release terms. And then I would have to formally agree to it; agree to paying the money I owed. The condition was that I had to pay back the full amount within a month.

It was terrifying. How the hell was I going to pay it back? There was no way I could do that – it was something that had been constantly running through my mind ever since he first mentioned it. But of course I would agree to it. If it meant I was free, of course I would say I'd pay it. He told me again about the other conditions of my release, how I had to advertise Black Death in the UK media. I would be paid for interviews, he said, and I could give Black Death the money for it. 'Killing two birds with one stone,' he said.

It was around 6pm when the letter came through. MD had been doing lots of email checks throughout the afternoon but nothing had been sent. He would go downstairs, go outside to check and come back and say, 'Still nothing.' I started to think the letter wouldn't come at all. I felt my body get tense with nerves and anticipation and I fully expected to be told that they had changed their minds. Every time he came through those beads and nothing had come through I swear a bit of me died. He was convinced the letter would come, so that did help me a bit, but I was still certain that now I had got so close, something would go wrong. I don't know why I thought like that, why I wasn't trying to stay positive. I couldn't bring myself to have such hope.

The doors stayed open until it got dark and I felt energised by having them open. I wanted to stay out there until the last moment. But then, as we were going in, my eyes looked down to the outhouse building and I was reminded of the grim fate of other girls. Had they really been kept there, handcuffed and gagged before…I didn't want to think about it. Suddenly the landscape, however magnificent and breath-taking, couldn't disguise the ugly truth of that evil reality. An evil that existed in even the most beautiful place.

Then the letter of release came through from CK. CK

wanted MD to confirm with me that I accepted the terms of payment. It was actually written in the letter that he had told me. And if I didn't pay? If I couldn't pay? The death penalty. It said, 'any disobedience with any of the above will result in your *elimination*'. That was the scariest part. Even though I was going to be free tomorrow, I wouldn't be really free until I had paid money I didn't have.

You know what I thought then? I honestly thought, at that point, at least I will see my family for a bit. At least I will have a month with them and then I will die. Any time was better than nothing. Seeing them again, even for a moment, would be better than not seeing them. I was so grateful that I might get a month to be with them, to spend time with them, to love them. I could cope with that. I could die after that.

Here is the letter in full, complete with grammatical errors:

You are being released as a huge generosity from Black Death Group. You release does, however, come with a warning and you should read this letter carefully.

You are certainly aware of your value on human slavery market and must make a note that this isn't personal, this is business. For your release we have taken a number of factors into consideration.

A mistake was made by capturing you, especially considering you are a young mother that should have in no circumstances be lured into kidnapping. Second important factor you are very well aware of is your overall protection by one of our main and very well respected men who made a clear and solid stance in your case.

You will, upon your landing in your home country, cease any investigation activities related to your kidnapping. You also agree to sneak a predetermined set of information in to the media and we will expect to see evidence that has been done in the near future.

You and your family will in no way ever talk about us in bad language and without respect. You have been treated fairly, with respect, and we expect to hear exactly the same about us in return. You can release any information you have heard from MD while your holding as he would never give you any information that could harm our activities. We will not tolerate lying about anything that has happened.

You have also agreed to pay outstanding costs of your release of $50,000. We expect that money to be paid in BitCoins within one month. Any sort of disobedience with the above will result in your elimination.

He showed me the letter on the laptop and read through it with me. I wanted some sort of confirmation that once I was finally free and I'd paid them then I wouldn't be touched again and it would be all over. I really wanted that. He said he would try to get that for me. Once I had paid it, he said, a letter or email would come through. Or a courier would put something through my door.

'No!' I said, 'No, no, I don't want that. I don't want them to come close to my house, to my family.'

'They know where you live,' he said darkly. We can find out where anyone lives. I knew that. If I paid it and did all the other things I had to do I would be free. They would put me on that 'untouchable' list and that would be it. This would all be over. They would have the money and the publicity and I would have done what I needed to do.

It sounds so business-like, doesn't it? How would you feel about being on the 'do not touch' list of the biggest crime organisation of the world? MD kept asking me this. He was saying it like it was going to be a massive achievement. He wanted me to feel grateful to be on the list, like it was my goal. At some points I really did feel that. How weird is that now? For that to be my goal. My aim.

There was another thing I had to do, and for MD this was the point he kept stressing the most. When I landed back in the UK, when I got off the plane, the first thing I had to do was end any sort of police investigation that had started. He was adamant I had to make this my number one priority. 'Don't even go home – go straight to the police and end the investigation,' he said. 'Don't answer any questions. They will ask you questions and they will push you and try and make you talk but just say no.'

'OK,' I said. 'But the money…the money is the biggest issue for me. I don't know how I'm going to pay that—' He cut me off. He was starting to get quite agitated now.

'No, that isn't the biggest thing. The biggest thing is the police. Stop any questions, stop any investigation.' He was deadly serious. I was in no doubt about what I had to do. I had to reassure him I would do this for him. I would then be free and he would be free from Black Death. And I knew that he wouldn't change his mind overnight; he had something to get excited about and it kept him in a good mood.

But my question still remained: the letter stated I had to pay in Bitcoins. I didn't even know what they were. He explained I needed to find a Bitcoin dealer but I had no idea how. He would help me, he said. He would go behind Black Death's back and help me. This would be the worst-case scenario. I had to try and get as much as I could but he would help me, he said.

He started talking about the plan for the following day, and what he intended to do with me on my release. He was going to drive us to the consulate. Well, he said he would drop me about twenty minutes away, so I would have to walk in by myself. He was going to dump the car, let someone steal it and then drive off in one of his other cars – a Maserati, he said. There would be no tracing him, he said.

It was about 10pm when he turned off the lights that night. He had set his phone for 4am as it was such a long drive and he wanted to leave early. He wanted to get a good sleep, he said, and then rolled over. I tried to get to sleep too but I just couldn't. I kept thinking, what if something goes wrong? Everything was so prepared, what if something happens at the last minute that messes it all up? What if the alarm doesn't go off or if he gets an email in the morning and CK has changed his mind? My mind wouldn't turn off. I could taste freedom and yet I wasn't sure if it would actually happen. I knew I had to do everything he asked me to do, otherwise Black Death would kill me.

I probably managed a few hours' sleep in the end. I kept

thinking of my Ashton, kissing his cheeks... Would I see him tomorrow? Would they fly me straight home? I would see my mum, and Nylah would be so pleased to see me. I could just picture her waiting for me. I closed my eyes. Tomorrow I will be free. Tomorrow I will be free.

CHAPTER 10

Freedom…but not free

'"Do you have an appointment?" a woman's voice spoke back. "No," I said, "it's an emergency."'

MONDAY 17 July

The alarm was set for 4am and I was straight out of the bed when it went off. It was pitch black but I was so happy. I hadn't slept much; everything that was meant to happen was playing through my head. Would I ever really leave this place? Would I ever really see my mum and Ashton again or was it just all too good to be true? I wanted to be so happy. I wanted to believe it would happen. The minute I woke up the countdown had begun. How long would it be until I saw my family? How long would it be until I was saved?

I had slept in one of the T-shirts MD had given me and I went to put my pink bodysuit back on. Since that first shower when I had taken it off, it had stayed in the corner

129

of the bedroom. Discarded, abandoned. I couldn't wait to take it off then and yet now... I couldn't wait to put it back on. Don't get me wrong, it was grimy, it was dirty, it had dried sweat all over it and it smelt unpleasant, but it was a reminder of who I was. It was my piece of clothing, it was feminine, not something I had been given in captivity. It was mine. I had packed it on the Monday evening before I flew to Milan. I had chosen it as something I wanted to wear to a photo shoot on Tuesday morning when I would be modelling motorbike leathers and then going home for a brief pit-stop before flying to Ibiza. That wasn't me, was it? That seemed like such a long time ago. Was it even real?

I stepped into the bodysuit and remembered the last time I had put it on – fresh that morning, excited, ready to shoot. Now, strangely, it was equally exciting to put it back on. I was ready to have control again. I was ready to be Chloe again. I put on the tracksuit top and trousers over the top and slipped on the trainers. I didn't need to unlace them – they were too big. But they were so much better than those slider things, and I needed something to walk to the consulate in. MD was up and changing too.

He left the room first and the beads rattled as he walked through. I will never hear those beads again, I thought. I looked back at the bed and my red blanket. It had kept me warm and it had protected me from getting more bitten than I had. It was mine. But it wasn't mine. Nothing here was. This wasn't me, but I was getting back to me.

We went down to the kitchen. He pulled out a huge wad of cash from his pocket and made a big show of flashing it around so I saw it. I watched as he took a few notes from the stash.

'I will only need this much now,' he said. He left the rest behind on the table. I was scared about walking twenty minutes to the consulate by myself after he had dropped me off. What if someone else from Black Death got to me in that time? He would order me a taxi, he said, from where he dropped me off. He would take extra money for the taxi.

He was coming back later; I wasn't. I wasn't ever coming back. Or so I told myself. I had to believe it.

We went outside to the darkness. It was still; everything was silent apart from that typical insect noise. The crickets were loud but I couldn't see them, as it was all black. I could see the outhouse building's silhouette in the torchlight as MD made his way down the path.

'You get lots of mice here,' he said, and waved his torch around as if he was looking for them. When we'd driven to the village the previous day he'd said to keep my eye out for wild cats on the mountain road. I hadn't seen any, and I didn't see any mice that morning. I made myself concentrate on the pathway. I didn't want to think about that place.

He was using the torch from his phone as I tried to follow him as closely as I could and use his light. I didn't want to trip up and hurt myself. I didn't want anything to go wrong. I couldn't go back to this – I had to keep safe, I had to keep going. We made our way carefully down the path. It wasn't cold but I held my arms round my chest as we walked.

We got to the car and he opened the door for me. I sat inside. MD turned to me.

'Did you ever think I was lying to you?' he asked. 'Did you ever think that I was just telling you you would be released but then you never would?' He was staring at me.

I couldn't quite believe what I was hearing. Why the hell was he saying this now? Alarm bells were ringing in my head as he spoke. Was this a trick? Why would he say this to me now?

'No,' I said. 'I believed you.' I didn't want to show any sense of doubt, any sign that I didn't trust him at all. I did trust him, I told him. I wanted all thoughts of him not releasing me out of his head.

CK had tricked a girl before, he said. CK had told a girl he was going to release her after keeping her prisoner. She thought she was being released and he took her to the car to pretend to take her home and then told her it was all a trick. She was then taken away to be sold.

He spoke so calmly. I didn't know what to say to that. Why was he telling me this now? It was like when he told me he would poison food as a method of killing people. He told me that right before he brought me some food to eat. It was like he wanted to control how scared I was. He could instil fear; he had that power. I waited. I held my breath. He seemed satisfied with what he had told me. He turned away and typed the postcode of the consulate into the satnav. He showed me he was putting it in. He told me, look, see, I'm not tricking you, and said it would take about four hours to get there.

I put my seat back and wound down the window. I wanted the fresh air to keep me awake. I wanted him to think that I trusted him completely, that I never doubted him. I never slept; I kept my eyes shut most of the journey to appear relaxed but I wasn't ever asleep. I kept checking we were following the satnav, that we weren't suddenly going somewhere else. There was no way I wanted to fall asleep. I had to be alert. Adrenaline was pumping through me and I felt so tense. Nearly there, I told myself, nearly there.

We made good time. We arrived by 7.30am and it was light by the time we got there. The consulate didn't open until 9.30am, so his original plan of dropping me off to let me walk the last twenty minutes and head straight in wasn't going to work. He didn't want to leave me for two hours by myself, he said, and I made it clear I didn't want to be left for that length of time in case another Black Death member saw him. I felt safe with him. He parked the car in a car park next to the consulate and we went to a cafe, which was right next door. MD went for a table in the corner.

There are so many things I can remember clearly but can I tell you if I ate anything in that cafe? I genuinely can't remember. I think I had some orange juice and a croissant. I think MD had the same. It seems so trivial, having breakfast. But I didn't want to upset him now. I couldn't afford to upset him. Even though I knew he would take me to the consulate, there were thousands of Black Death agents around. I had to pay the money I owed otherwise I would be killed. I was relying on MD to get me through that, to help me. What if I couldn't pay straight away or there was a delay in paying him, or I missed a deadline? I had to keep him on my side as he was the only one who might be able to stop them taking action against me.

Music played in the background, and it was so surreal to hear music after all this time. It felt so normal. The cafewas filling up with customers, as it was morning rush hour. Everyone looked so smartly dressed. We were in the centre of Milan and everyone was going off to work. I felt so self-conscious of how I looked. He told me that when we were in the village the previous day he had overheard a girl talking to her friend. 'Look at her,' the girl had said, referring to me apparently. I felt even more self-conscious now with so many people around.

While we were in the cafe he made sure I knew his new plan. He went over and over and over it with me. He kept checking his phone to see if it was nearly 9.30am. He told me what he wanted me to do when we got in there. He said he would come into the consulate with me but I had to say he was a friend. I had to tell the authorities that when I was released by my kidnappers in the middle of nowhere, I had gone up to a random person and asked them to use their phone. I then called MD's number, as I knew it by heart as he was the only person I knew in Italy. I knew he was living in Italy and he would be able to help me. That is what he wanted me to say. That was the story that he wanted me to tell. I then had to tell them that he came to rescue me from the outskirts of Milan, where I was dumped, and that he brought me here, to the safety of the consulate. He would be coming in with me, he told me, he would be right there with me. He was almost certain I would get a flight home that night. He was sure of it.

And then he gave me his business card. It was a white card and, in the middle, printed with black ink, were the words 'Permanent Solution'. Above the writing there was a picture of the Grim Reaper. I turned the card over and on the back was his email address, printed across the middle. It was his email address from the dark web. I can remember the words: MD@...and then something else. It was a really complicated email address. This was my method of contacting him afterwards, he said. This was how I could get hold of him to give him the money for Black Death.

Now I was in a cafe right next door to the consulate, I felt confident asking him again how I was meant to get Bitcoins and find a Bitcoin dealer. I was out of the house now; we were in central Milan, and he couldn't 'keep' me any longer. He told me he would catch a ferry to the UK. He would bring lots of cash that way rather than by plane, which would arouse suspicion. He would help me get the money changed into Bitcoin. We sat there until his phone said 9.20am and he announced it was time to go. This was it.

★ ★ ★

The British Consulate didn't look like the magnificent building I had been expecting. In fact, it hadn't been exactly easy to find — MD had struggled at first to find it on the street. I don't know what I was expecting...something grand, maybe? You could only tell what it was from the flag flying from the top of the building. There were two or three rows of glass windows running just below. This was it.

We went through the doors. The consulate wasn't on the ground floor so, again, we had to wait to be allowed up. It must be nearly 9.30am, and I thought the wait shouldn't be too long. We sat down on the seats by the ground-floor reception for a few minutes. I saw other people starting to go through the doors, then to the lifts, so we followed suit. We got into the lift. It said the consulate was on the fifth floor. We rode up in silence and then the doors opened. There were two armed soldiers waiting, standing right in front of us.

It was nice to see them, in a way, and I should have felt safe, but I didn't. I was safe for the time being, I thought, but not for ever.

Past the soldiers were two big doors. There was an intercom by the side of one and we went over. MD was standing right behind me and told me to say, 'It's an emergency.' He whispered it to me. I had been so used to relying on him and doing everything he said the past few days and, even now, even at the consulate, he was still in control. I pressed the button and waited for a response.

'I need to speak in private,' I said. I think my voice broke a bit then. There were other people behind us. 'Do you have an appointment?' a woman's voice spoke back.

'No, it's an emergency. I want to talk in private.'

The doors buzzed and were opened for us. In front of us now was a waiting room with a counter and windows above it, so someone could sit behind the windows and see through. There was a security frame too, like you get at airports, and we had to go through that first. We walked through and MD whispered to me, 'I knew they would have one of these.' It was as if he was saying he was still in control. He hadn't come armed with his knife because he knew security measures would be in place. Nothing surprises him, he was boasting.

We sat down on the chairs. I could see two ladies behind the desk now. One of them looked at me and then back at the other lady, a blonde lady, and I heard her say, 'That's her, the one in the tracksuit.' The blonde lady came to the window. She looked about forty years old. Her name was Nicoletta. She was the first person I had spoken to other than MD for days; the first face I had seen properly for days. I looked at her and heard myself speak.

'I was kidnapped.' My first words. She looked me in the eyes and asked me to confirm my name. I said Chloe. Nicoletta told me later that she wasn't allowed to say, 'Are you Chloe?' even though she knew I was. She had to let me identify myself to make sure.

She looked at MD. 'Who is that?' she asked, and I said he was a friend. He turned to me. 'Time to put these on,' he said, as he took out his sunglasses. It was really weird. I turned back to Nicoletta.

'I need to take you through to a private room now,' she said.

'I'm coming with her,' said MD.

'You aren't allowed,' she said. She was firm, matter-of-fact. He insisted that he had to come. 'I have to be with her,' he said. He obviously didn't trust me that I wouldn't tell Nicoletta he was just a friend. Why else would he insist in trying to come in with me to a private room?

She repeated, 'You aren't allowed.'

When he realised she wasn't going to change her mind, he said to me, 'OK, I'm going now. You have the email.' But Nicoletta wasn't going to let him go. 'No, stop. We need you here,' she said to him.

She opened a door through to a private room. I was patted down and searched by another woman as I went through some double doors and then into a big meeting room. We sat down together and I briefly explained what had happened to me. I told her I had been taken at a photo shoot, then drugged and put in a car. I told her about being kept at the house. I started to cry then. The relief of telling someone what had happened to me was immense.

She was very calm and told me she knew who I was. She said they had called the police now and they would be on their way. She was very kind and spoke very good English. Hearing that the police were coming was meant to be the best feeling in the world, but how could I be happy when I knew I wasn't allowed to talk to them because Black Death had forbidden it? MD hadn't thought that the police in Italy would question me. He thought I would be released and sent back to the UK, where I would be able to say nothing. No comment, that was it; I was meant to stop any investigation.

Nicoletta gave me a bottle of water. She sat next to me and waited for me to stop crying, then guided me out of the private room. The police had arrived. We went out through the double doors and back to the waiting room of the consulate. The door into the waiting room kept opening and closing. I watched as the police came in and out of it. They were in plain clothes and had surrounded MD. I could see all this as the door opened and closed. One of them was studying what looked like the ID card he'd showed me in the house; the one with his fake name. He told me at the time that he'd destroyed it. He had made a big show of going out, telling me he was going to burn it. I looked at him now. He was surrounded; he was shaking his head. I didn't know what was happening to him but the way he was shaking his head he must have thought I had told the police he was the kidnapper, even though I hadn't said anything.

He looked at me and it was a look that said, 'Don't say anything.' I could see him so clearly and I was petrified. If the police had him, who would I contact about paying back Black Death? He was the only one who could help me. He was the only one who could protect me from being killed.

Lots of police officers came over to me and asked me who he was. I said, 'He is a friend. I called him from a stranger's phone.' I was repeating exactly what MD had told me to say. One of the policemen asked me what his number was. Of course, I didn't know. They knew I didn't know. 'I can't think straight,' I said. I shook my head and shrugged.

It was time to go to the police station. Nicoletta asked me if I wanted her to come to the station with her and I did. She wasn't allowed to be my interpreter as she worked at the consulate, but she acted as an unofficial one until one was found. She walked next to me and the two other police officers walked either side. They walked me into the lift, past where MD was still surrounded. It was to be the last time I saw him properly. We went down and out of the building and got into a big police car. They put the sirens on and held a sign out of the window while they were driving, I think to get past everyone. We were travelling so fast. I was safe for the moment but, I knew, not for ever. Even if they got MD and the other guys who were involved in my kidnapping, it was physically impossible to get everyone in Black Death. They couldn't get all of them, I thought. I was physically free, but I couldn't be free from all of them. In my mind I was still a prisoner.

CHAPTER 11

Safe

'They took my fingerprints and took photos of my ankles and wrists. I provided a urine test and a hair sample for the doctor. My hair sample showed traces of Ketamine, the powerful horse tranquilliser. That was the drug the kidnappers had used to knock me out.'

We arrived at the police station in a matter of moments. Well, that's what it felt like. The journey there was fast and, when I stepped out of the car, I looked up at what I thought was a castle. It was a huge brick building with two towers either side and I could see two guards on the door as we got closer. Nicoletta was right by my side as we walked through and I was guided to a waiting room where the officers were milling around. Was I OK? Did I need anything? There were lots of people asking me questions. I got a sense of being looked at but in a covert manner. A female officer came over and checked if I was OK. She told me I was beautiful. Then it was time to go through to an interview room. There were two people behind a desk in the room, one typing on a computer. These were the two main investigators and they introduced themselves as Serena Ferrari and Gianluca Simontacci. Gianluca did most of the typing as I talked. They told me they were going to ask me some questions and I would have to reply with what I could remember.

For the next fifteen hours I sat in that room and answered the questions as best I could. I answered them all, every single one. They had no idea that by answering, by telling them everything, I was sentencing myself to death. I was doing what I had to do but I knew I was going to die because of it. I was going against what MD had told me and broken the rules of being released, but I couldn't not answer. I told them everything I could remember. I was telling them everything that MD had told me. I told them about his role in Black Death, I told them what he earned, and what he told me happened to other girls who were kidnapped. I wasn't going to hold back. I wasn't going to stop answering.

Can I remember the very first question I was asked? I have no idea. The process was that they would ask Nicoletta a question, she would translate it for me and I would answer her in English. She would then translate it back to them and they would ask the next question. I remember there being lots of coffee…lots and lots of coffee was brought into the room. And Nicoletta stayed with me the whole time.

At some point during the day a doctor turned up. The

police explained and Nicoletta translated that she would take samples from me. The puncture wound on my arm was looked at under a microscope and recorded and analysed. My wrists were still sore and they were examined. They took my fingerprints and took photos of my ankles and wrists. I provided a urine test and a hair sample for the doctor. I had to take my hair down and they pushed it forward to cut a large chunk from the back. It was so knotted and such a mess, all over my face. The urine sample showed no traces of any drug but my hair sample showed traces of ketamine, the powerful horse tranquilliser. That was the drug the kidnappers had used to knock me out.

Halfway through the questioning they decided that Nicoletta wasn't allowed to be my interpreter any more, as she worked for the consulate. So they brought in a new one, but this new woman wasn't as good, as her English wasn't as fluent. It meant everything seemed to take a lot longer. Nicoletta stayed with me but I found I had to keep repeating myself a lot and it was exhausting. I could see it getting darker and darker outside. By the end I couldn't keep my eyes open.

It was around 1am when the prosecutor joined us. He had been in at the beginning of my interview to introduce himself and tell me I would have to stay in Milan for a few days. He told me he had spoken to the shoe lady. I honestly didn't understand who he meant at first. My mind drew a blank. He wanted to know why I hadn't mentioned getting the shoes before. He asked me a few questions and I answered everything straight away, all his questions. Of course, it probably looks weird that I didn't talk about getting the shoes but it really was as simple as that. To me they had no relevance. I couldn't understand why it was suddenly a big deal. Of course, they had to explore all sides of the story and I had no problem explaining the whole trip to the village when I was specifically asked about it.

To some people it may seem strange that I didn't try to escape, but no one understands the depths of brainwashing I underwent by MD. I can't tell you how mentally exhausted I was, and it was at that moment the prosecutor asked how could he be expected to believe anything else I said? I was shocked. It hadn't crossed my mind that people wouldn't believe me. I had just spent hours describing everything in detail. I was exhausted. I was trying to remember everything and yet for him to still doubt me...

I started to cry. I was remembering every detail I could, even though MD had told me not to. I had been up since 4am. It was like my worst nightmare. After all of this, I just wanted to get home. I just wanted to go home, I said. I wanted to see my son and my mum and my dog. I couldn't believe it; it seemed just too much.

By the time the police had finished with the questions it was 3am and they wanted me to go to a safe house for the next few days. I wanted Nicoletta to come with me; I didn't want her to leave me. She was so kind and she spoke good English and it was comforting to have her with me.

We left the police station and I was driven to the safe house. There were no sirens this time, but it wasn't far away. We got there about 3.30am. The safe house turned out to be sheltered accommodation. There was a young woman in a little office. I sat in there and cried. She tried to comfort me but I couldn't be comforted. Once you entered you weren't allowed to come out, for your own protection. That is the way it was put to me – they used the words 'inmates' and 'not allowed to leave'. I couldn't believe it. I had just been held captive and now I was being held again in this safe house. I couldn't bear it; it was just horrific.

Why did I stay there? The prosecutor was worried I might escape. But I couldn't go anywhere anyway – I had no money, no clothes and no passport! During the police interview, Nicoletta had gone out to get me some clothes and toiletries. She had bought me a black T-shirt and jogging bottoms, toothbrush and toothpaste. I carried them into the safe house now, in a plastic bag, and was shown up to my room by this really old-looking man. The hostel was a mess. Everywhere I looked there was rubbish in bags left along the hallways, and there was such a horrible, horrible smell to the place. When we got to my room the man told me I would be sharing with two other girls, who were both sleeping on their beds. There were three single beds and the middle one was empty. That was my bed. There were windows at the top right of the wall, next to the beds, but the room was dark. To the left was a toilet and a shower.

Everyone there was a victim of crime but it felt like a punishment being held there. I looked at the sleeping girls. There was a black girl one side and a white girl the other side. They were both fast asleep and I didn't want to wake them but I was desperate to get out of the tracksuit MD had given me, so I went and had a shower. There was no lock on the door but I didn't think I would be disturbed at that time of the morning. And at that point I didn't care.

I climbed into the bed and under the thin blanket. The mattress was lumpy and, as I lay there, I felt like crying again. I remembered lying in bed at the farmhouse only twenty-four hours earlier and picturing what would happen when I was free. I imagined I would be on a flight home straight away, that they would see I needed to be with my family, that I had suffered enough and that I was in need of my mum and my son. But I honestly couldn't believe what was happening.

It's only for a few days, I told myself. I'll be home soon. Only a few days. But I was powerless to leave. I was trapped again.

I woke up the next morning and saw that the clock on the wall said 11am. When I sat up properly I could see my roommates had gone. I had heard them wake up and get up and move around the room earlier that morning but I'd pretended I was still asleep. Now the light was coming into the room and I wanted to see what was happening, what was going on.

I got dressed in the new clothes Nicoletta had bought me and went out of the room. Do you know how it felt? It honestly felt like I was in a mental hospital. I stood by my door and watched a girl walking along the corridor. She looked like a zombie. She didn't look at me, just straight ahead, and was pacing up and down the corridor. Up and down without a word. I moved past her and went into a biggish room that had a table and chairs and more girls inside. There were a couple of Chinese girls sitting at a table doing something with some small plastic beads. They were passing them from one hand to another and then putting them in tubs. They looked like robots, they were doing it so methodically, so mechanically. It looked so creepy.

One woman came over to me to say hello. She spoke a bit of English and told me her name. 'Welcome,' she said. I started to cry. There was just no reason not to any more. I was free but I had Black Death watching me and I wasn't allowed to go home and see my mum. I wanted to find the old man who'd showed me to my room last night and see if he could contact Nicoletta for me. I wanted to speak to my mum; I was desperate to speak to her. All these thoughts, all these things were running through my mind and eventually it got too much. I was openly crying in front of strangers. I couldn't help it or I didn't care. Probably a bit of both. What is my life in this place? I thought. I went back to my room, back to my bed, in tears.

★ ★ ★

Probably the worst part of that day was not knowing what was happening. I hadn't been told by the police or prosecutor what was happening and, even though I believed Nicoletta when she told me she was coming today, I didn't know when that would be. I didn't know anything. At lunchtime, everyone went into the bigger room and they served a pasta dish that wasn't particularly appealing but I ate a bit. After everyone had finished I saw the people serving it gather everyone's plates and scrape the leftover pasta back into the serving pot. They were going to serve it again the next day. I felt so sick.

I spent most of the rest of the day back in my room trying to sleep to kill time. Nicoletta came later that afternoon and I had never been so pleased to see her. I went downstairs to meet her and we went into another room to talk. There was no air con in this place either. I had got used to it but Nicoletta commented on how hot it was. I explained about the poor conditions and she wanted to take a look for herself.

'Can I come upstairs?' she asked. She couldn't believe the bin bags in the corridor, mixed in with the heat; the smell was disgusting. She called the prosecutor to check if he would allow me access to a hotel. I kept everything crossed that he would and he did.

While she was on the phone to him, they asked me for the password for my phone. The police told me when I first saw them at the consulate that they had been to the studio, the site of my abduction, and found my belongings there. On the Wednesday after my abduction, Phil had received the email at 10.34am with my ransom demand from Black Death and reported it to the police in Italy and British Consulate in Milan. The investigation into finding me had been launched straight away and the police went to the studio in Milan after getting details from Phil. They found my clothes, suitcase and phone, all abandoned. Now they wanted me to unlock my phone for further investigations.

There was part of me, when hearing that, that felt a huge relief. I had known when I spent that first night handcuffed to the chest of drawers that people would be looking for me. I had known they would be doing all they could to find me. I was grateful to hear the amount of effort and the number of people behind the investigation. I gave the password to Nicoletta and asked her to thank the prosecutor. I was so happy to be leaving this place. But where would I go? I didn't want to be far from Nicoletta, from the police. I wanted to be near to everyone, to as many people I could. She suggested a hotel called the Duomo Apartments, which were right next to the consulate, so I would feel safe. It was perfect.

★ ★ ★

We had to call Phil, as he had to book the hotel for me. I had no other way of doing it. I had no choice. Nicoletta called him and I spoke to him. He was so shocked to hear my voice. I could tell he was shocked even though everyone in the UK had been informed I had been released the moment I arrived at the consulate.

He recognised my voice. He asked me about the hotel and said he would book it for two nights. He didn't want to book any more as we didn't know how long I would be in Italy and, at that point, I thought it would only be a couple of nights maximum. I told him it was the Duomo Apartments, by the consulate. The consulate is right next to the Duomo, a beautiful big cathedral. It is the largest church in Italy and just incredible to see. And these apartments were right there.

Nicoletta left me some euros for a taxi and I went back up to my room to get my things. When I came back down I asked the lady at the front desk to come with me over the road to the taxi rank. She could understand enough English to do this. I didn't want to leave the building alone. What if someone from Black Death was watching me? I was clutching my bag of belongings and I only had to take a few steps from the door to the car, but I didn't want to go alone, which is why I asked the lady if she could come with me. Could she take me to the taxi? I am twenty years old but I was so frightened in that moment, of being alone, of going out alone, that I needed help. So she did. I was petrified, but I knew I had to do it. The taxi took me straight to the apartments and the car door was right by the entrance. There was a guy sitting behind the reception desk and I went straight up, telling him: 'Phil's made a booking.' It must have sounded strange but I just wanted to get to the safety of my room.

'Have you got any ID?' he asked me. Such a normal question when you check into a hotel, yet I had nothing. I looked like I had just come off the streets – at least I'm sure that was what he was thinking. I had my stuff in a paper bag. The police had given me a photocopy of my passport but that was it. That was all I had.

'What is this?' he asked. He looked at me again. I looked dodgy, of course I did. He was very reluctant to even look at my booking. So I started to explain why I had a photocopy of my passport, why I had no suitcase, just a paper bag. Why I was so nervous. I knew he wasn't going to let me in otherwise. So I started explaining and he couldn't believe what had happened to me. He was actually very nice.

'I am so sorry,' he said. He introduced himself as Carlo, the owner of the apartments. He took me up to my room and it took my breath away. It was so nice. There were two double beds in the room, a kitchen area, a beautiful bathroom. And best of all? It was on the same road as the consulate.

Carlo, the guy on reception, became an extra level of security for me. Every evening he would call up to my room and ask me what I wanted for dinner, then order me a takeaway. We had a code too. If he was bringing up food, he would always ring the room first. It was so I knew he was on his way. Otherwise I would be scared to answer the door – it could be anyone, I thought. He changed my name on the computer system too. He trusted his staff, he said, but it didn't hurt to keep it private. He wouldn't tell anyone my room number unless he knew them or had seen identification first.

That first evening he brought me up a pizza. It was different to any other pizza I had ever had. It was one massive slice, really thick and cut into squares. It was from Spontini and it was amazing. I had lost so much weight. I wasn't hungry but I *was* hungry. It was like my body had forgotten that sensation – but eating that pizza was the most comforting feeling ever.

Going to sleep that night was amazing. I wanted to make sure the door was locked but I already felt a sense of security with Carlo and from being so near the consulate. And I fell asleep that night, for the first time in over a week, feeling positive.

★ ★ ★

The next morning Nicoletta came for me and told Carlo that she was taking me shopping. I needed a bra and I knew she was coming but I hadn't warned Carlo. He interrogated her thoroughly, she later told me! He checked her ID and called the consulate to check she was who she said she was. He was very strict about it, she said. He told her that a friend of his had been kidnapped in South Africa and he knew how these people worked – he wanted to check everyone who said they were coming to see me. When he rang up to say a woman called Nicoletta was here, I of course told him it was fine. But I knew for sure from that point onwards that I was being looked out for.

Nicoletta's face was a picture when I saw her. 'What the hell?' she said, and I knew she was bemused by Carlo's extensive security checks. I felt so safe with him there. When he stayed at the hotel overnight, he stayed in the room next to me. I was on the first floor and there was a corridor of rooms and he was at the end. It was so reassuring to think he was there.

A few days after I first arrived, his brother came – a man called Filippo. He would stay in the room next to me if he was working and he was equally kind. They both lived in Rome and would alternate coming to Milan to work on the reception desk. They wouldn't normally work on Reception but it was holiday season in Milan and a lot of their staff were away. There was always someone on the reception desk, twenty-four hours a day, seven days a week.

It would usually be one of them but sometimes other staff were on the front desk. It was those people that worried me: they could be bribed, they could be given money to give up my room number – but when Carlo or Filippo were there, it was different.

The first weekend I spent in Carlo and Filippo's apartments, they both had to go back to Rome. That was the worst feeling ever. My haven was no longer 100 per cent safe. I still had fear at the back of my mind. What if Black Death bribed someone for the master key? During that weekend, I had a knock on my door when I wasn't expecting anyone. Even when he went to Rome, Carlo would order me dinner and he kept to the same routine – someone would call me just before the delivery driver arrived outside my door. But that evening I had already eaten. I wasn't expecting anyone else and there was a knock at my door. I rang Filippo straight away and he called Reception to find out what was going on. Apparently the receptionist told him he had made a mistake and he had knocked on my door by accident. But I wasn't convinced. How can you get the wrong door when the numbers are on them clear as day? I was paranoid. Psychologically I was frightened of Black Death now more than ever before. They would have known I had disobeyed one of their conditions of release, as one of their well-respected members was in police custody.

CHAPTER 12

Facing my fear

'"Hello?" was all she needed to say. I just broke down.'

I didn't speak to my mum until the third day after my release, the Thursday. I knew she knew I was safe. The police had told her, and everyone in the UK, that I had been released. They told me when I was at the consulate that my mum had been informed. It wasn't that I didn't want to speak to her; I just wasn't strong enough. I was holding back from her. I knew that, as soon as I heard her voice, I would break down. My reality was that I could only use a public phone to speak to her. I didn't have my own phone – I didn't actually get that back until I was back in the UK – and I knew I would get upset. I hate getting upset in public, so I was delaying it. I was faltering about making the call.

But mums know you better than you think, don't they? They have a funny way of knowing everything about their children. She understood without speaking to me why I wouldn't be calling her straight away. She knows me so well, and she would know why I hadn't called her until that point. People she knew kept telling her how weird it was that I hadn't called, but she knew why. At the police station, on Monday, they had asked me if I wanted to call her. I couldn't then. It was all too much that day. And at the apartment, I could have used the phone in the lobby.

* * *

After Nicoletta finished getting her grilling from Carlo on Wednesday, she took me shopping. We went to the high street to get a bra and then went straight back to the apartment. I didn't really like being out all that much, even though Nicoletta was with me. I just wanted to know what was going on. The frustrating thing was, at this point Nicoletta didn't know what was happening either. She didn't understand why I had to stay in Milan; she and her colleagues had asked the public prosecutor why I had to stay but hadn't been given any answers. They – by which I mean the consulate – were going to issue me with an emergency travel document, as I didn't have a passport, but the public prosecutor denied it. Not knowing why or what was going on or how long I would have to stay in Italy was devastating. I wanted to go home. I just wanted to see Mum and Ashton. I knew I had to call her. Sod the fact that everyone would see me cry, I had to speak to her. So I did. On Thursday, three days after I had been released, I spoke to Mum.

I called her from the consulate.

'Hello,' was all she needed to say. I just broke down. I could no longer hold in my emotions. It suddenly hit me – I was alive! And I was talking to my wonderful mum. I was OK. But I was hit with a longing in my heart that I had never known before. An ache to see my mum, an ache to be back home, an ache to just make everything else go away and for this nightmare to finally end. It took me a while to speak but I knew she would have seen the Italian number come up on her mobile. She probably thought at first that it was someone from the consulate or the police or something. I don't think she was expecting it to be me.

I couldn't even say hello back for the first few moments, I was just too tearful. And she started to cry too. 'Chloe…' she said. She didn't even need to ask who it was.

I couldn't imagine what she had been going through from the moment she was told I was missing to that moment when I first spoke to her after nine days of no contact, given that we usually speak every day. After we had both stopped crying enough to talk, I started to explain briefly what had happened. She didn't know what had happened to me at all. The police in the UK, after telling her I had been kidnapped, didn't tell her anything else. She had heard from Phil about emails that had been sent, that I was up for sale, but she didn't know anything else. The police hadn't told her anything.

She kept saying to me: 'Chloe, it's exactly what happens in the films.' She watches all these horror films all the time and she was saying to the UK police, 'It's like the films.' But the police were trying to reassure her it wasn't. So as soon as I told her I had been drugged she started to cry. She had been under a false reassurance that it wasn't as bad as she was imagining. I knew she wanted to come and be with me but she didn't have a passport. And besides, at that point, I honestly believed I was coming home soon. It was only going to be a few days, the prosecutor had said, and it wouldn't be worth my mum flying out to see me if I was going to be flying back the very next day. What if she got out there and I was already on my way home? I understood that, of course I did, but it didn't stop me wishing more than anything else in the world that she could just be with me.

We probably spoke for only about twenty minutes but, in that time, my whole resolve collapsed. I felt a sudden hit of reality. Up to that point, the only person I had spoken to from the UK was Phil, and now I was hearing my mum's voice for the first time in over a week. I was so happy but so homesick too. It was almost worse hearing it than not hearing it. I knew now, more than ever, what was important in my life and that was my mum and my son.

And I knew who wasn't important at that point. I was so cross with Phil. He seemed to Mum to be the most unhelpful guy ever. The first night I was missing, she called him throughout the night – 10pm, 11pm, and then he told her that he goes to bed at 12.30am and she couldn't ring after that. I had gone missing and he was telling my mum she couldn't get answers because he was too busy sleeping? She asked him what time he woke up and he said, 'Whenever I want to.' Mum was frantic and she needed him to be more useful than that.

★ ★ ★

I saw Nicoletta every day that first week and, in the absence
of my mum, this was a huge comfort. Sometimes she would
come to me, sometimes I went to the consulate. The police
were busy, I knew; they were working twenty hours a day
on the case and they didn't get a lot of spare time to talk to
me. But they were always helpful if I needed them. They
took me to the Western Union to get money from the
UK. I had no ID with me so they had to come with me
and validate everything. They took with them my driving
licence but they couldn't return it back to me.

★ ★ ★

It was the Friday of that first week when everything changed
for me. I got given a phone, a small Samsung. It was a
government phone, and they didn't want me to ring out
on it all the time, but I was allowed to use it when I needed
to. It was a relief to have it. I could call Mum whenever I
wanted and it gave me a sense of freedom again. I didn't
have to ask to use the phone, I just did it.

I went to the consulate that Friday morning and Nicoletta
told me they were trying everything they could to get me
home that afternoon. They could issue me with an emergency
passport. I couldn't believe it. I was so excited! I knew they
were trying everything they could to get me home that day –
but when I went back in the afternoon for confirmation that
I could fly back to the UK I got the devastating news that the
prosecutor wouldn't allow me to leave for at least another

week. A week! I felt like someone had punched me in the stomach. I was so shell-shocked by it all.

They told me the police would visit my apartment that evening to tell me why. I just wanted to go home now. I was beyond any point of being helpful, of being understanding. I just wanted to go home. I hope that doesn't sound resentful. I knew the police were doing all they could to help me, as well as working on the investigation, but I just couldn't cope any more. Another week would mean it would be nearly seventeen days since I had led any sort of normal life. Seventeen days seems like such a short space of time, doesn't it? And yet in the space of less than three weeks, my life had changed beyond all recognition. Seventeen days for your whole world to change. OK, I thought to myself. Another week. I would do this. I could do this.

★ ★ ★

The police came to the apartment, as they said they would, on Friday afternoon. It was the two lead investigators, Serena Ferrari and Gianluca Simontacci, and the interpreter who had been used in the first interview. They told me briefly what was going to happen, and why I was still there. I wasn't prepared for what they were about to tell me. It was the two worst things I could have been told – that I would have to go back to the house and to the studio for identification purposes, and I would have to face my kidnapper in court and give evidence.

It took a while for that to sink in, mainly because I didn't want it to. All I wanted to do was go home and put this nightmare behind me and now I was faced with the reality that I would have to see MD again and that awful place – that house where I had been held prisoner. But I had to do these things in order to get my passport back and for the investigation to be concluded.

So that was Friday and then I had the whole weekend to process what I had been told. My mum was not happy that I had to go back to the house where I'd been held captive. She didn't want me to go near it. She thought something bad might happen, that Black Death would try to take me again. She was frantic with worry. I couldn't think about that yet though. I had to prepare for going to court and seeing MD again.

★ ★ ★

The following week, the UK consul came to Milan from Rome to see me. Her name was Ms McDougall and she was very kind. Nicoletta and I met her in a cafe and she strongly advised me to get legal advice. She explained that official things in Italy were different to how they worked in England, and you needed a lawyer to do everything for you: draw up documents, represent you in court, help get you home. That was the point she was making most clearly – in order for me to get home I needed a lawyer to help me. It was nice to speak to her and I felt reassured. I felt like I was getting back a bit of control. I had a purpose now. I needed to find a lawyer.

I told Filippo this when I got back to the apartment and he organised a meeting for me to see his lawyer. It was very kind of him but his lawyer turned out to be a more general, domestic lawyer. I needed someone who specialised in criminal law.

I returned to the consulate and went with Nicoletta to the office. She gave me a list of English-speaking Italian lawyers. I looked through it and the very top name was Francesco Pesce. I picked him because he specialised in only one thing: criminal law. In my mind that meant he was the best. He was the one. The consulate called him and he wanted to speak to me straight away. After a few minutes of chatting he said he thought it would be better to meet face to face, as it was quite a long conversation to have over the phone. I didn't want to go to his offices alone so I went with Nicoletta, who was happy to walk the ten minutes or so to his building. I couldn't go anywhere by myself. I would always want people with me, and she understood that and didn't try to make me go on my own.

It was Wednesday of the second week when I went to Francesco's office building. We were greeted by him and a trainee lawyer working for him. Nicoletta and I started explaining, quite briefly at first, what had happened to me. I didn't give away a massive amount of detail but he understood what had happened and he wanted to help me; he wanted to take on my case.

He pulled out this massive book. It was a book of law, he said, and he flicked through it briefly before telling me that the prosecutor had no right to take my passport without valid reason. And I hadn't been given a reason. The police had told me that I would have to go to court and visit the house and studio before I was allowed home, but I hadn't been told when that would be. So he said that he would go to the DA's office the next morning and try to find out what was going on. He was going to speed things up for me, he said, and it was so wonderful to hear that someone was on my side and helping me. His task was to get me home, and he wasn't worried about payment at that moment.

What sort of amazing lawyer is that? I was expecting someone who would want money up front and yet here was a man who actually said to me, in that first initial meeting, 'I am not worried about payment. My main task is to get you home.' He knew how important that was to me; how nothing else mattered at that point.

Of course, the subject of money did come up but Francesco explained I would only have to pay for any expenses he incurred. But I was adamant I didn't want him to just have expenses; I wanted him to have everything he deserved. He was so professional but also kind and genuine at the same time. I was so lucky to have him.

And he was true to his word – he fought my corner about going home and made it clear to the DA that my court appearance had to be in the first ten days of August otherwise I would be going home and would return later for the court date. The date was set for Friday 4 August. The house and studio visit was scheduled for the Wednesday 2 August, but on the Tuesday it got postponed until the Saturday. So it was now going to be after my court appearance. I couldn't tell you which one I was dreading more because they both gave me nightmares equally, but if

I was to see my mum and my son any time soon, I had to get through both ordeals.

★ ★ ★

It was hard though. And I did struggle with the thought of staying another week in Milan. After my initial meeting with Francesco, I thought he might be able to sort it out that I could go home and come back to face MD in court. But when he agreed a date with the DA of 4 August, fresh paperwork emerged that I had to sign. It said I would appear at court on that date and not leave the country before that. My dream of seeing my mum and son before enduring the court appearance was shattered and I didn't take the news well. I had a panic attack in my apartment the day the trainee lawyer came over to get me to sign it. I couldn't breathe. I couldn't see past the desperateness of not being allowed home. I refused to sign the document. I was in no fit state to do anything even though I knew deep down that signing the document meant the process was moving forward and I would be one step closer to home. It just didn't feel like that at the time.

The receptionist kept calling up to my apartment, telling me to come down. Francesco kept calling me, as the trainee lawyer downstairs had called him telling him I wasn't coming down. I just refused to answer the phone to anyone – the receptionist, Francesco… It was my own little battle. It was Nicoletta who came to my room in the end and spoke to me gently and calmed me down.

She encouraged me to go downstairs and told me I needed to sign the document as it was a step in the right direction.

She was the one who talked me into going downstairs and then to going with the lawyer to Francesco's office and signing the paperwork. We were meeting the police there too as they always checked that I was OK with whatever was happening.

I knew MD was in prison and that he would be held there until the court appearance. Francesco had told me that he had been badly beaten up by inmates when he first went inside. But to me, he was the guy who had saved me. He was the guy who was going to help me and if he was in jail that left me out here all by myself with hundreds of Black Death agents watching me and waiting for me. MD couldn't help me now. I knew by this point that his name wasn't Andre, and it wasn't MD either. I had seen some police documents with his real name, Lukasz Herba. No one had told me this. I just happened to see it. At this stage, knowing him as Lukasz and not by the Black Death initials didn't alter his status to me. He was still the only one in my mind who could help me.

It was now Thursday, the day before I was due to go to court. Both Francesco and Nicoletta were on holiday, although Francesco was due back the day after court – the day I was due to return to the house and studio. Simontacci came to visit me at the apartment building that afternoon. I will always remember his words. He said: 'No matter what happens in the next two days, you will be going home on Sunday.' I can't tell you how incredible that was to hear. I didn't want to believe it at first but he was adamant. He said that I could go ahead and book my flights for Sunday.

He told me he knew the truth behind the whole investigation and that I wouldn't have to be as fearful as I had been here when I was home in the UK. I would be able to go home on Sunday, he said again. Then he started to chat to Carlo in Italian. When Simontacci left, I asked Carlo what they were speaking about. He told me that Simontacci had made him aware it was only a matter of time now before the story of my kidnap went public. I was later told that this was what happened in Italy: a case of public interest is made public. The investigation was out in the open now. A press statement had been released and it wouldn't take long for the world's media to pick up on it. At that point I was still trying to process what Simontacci had said, his exact words: 'Truth behind the investigation'. What did that mean? I didn't know. I had a feeling, however, deep inside my gut, that I was about to find out in court. And it turned out I was right.

CHAPTER 13

The monster in court

'He said to me, "In May this year, did you know
Lukasz ordered two black ski masks online?"'

The court date was set for Friday 4 August. I was at the end
of my third week in Italy now although, having been told
that I could go home on Sunday, the end was at least in
sight. Francesco was due back from holiday later that day but
I now had the next best thing helping me: I had his mum,
Daria Pesce.

Daria is a well-respected lawyer in her own right, and I
liked her immediately. I had met her a couple of days before
the court date, when she went through Lukasz's statement
with me. She spoke good English and was able to interpret
it for me. And the interpretation was surreal. Lukasz had
related everything that had happened but he didn't mention
Black Death at all. Instead he said he was asked by some

167

Romanians from Birmingham to hire locations for storing garments. Well, as soon as I heard that my mind went into overdrive. This guy had never been to the UK; that's what he'd told me. Why would he say that?

It was all a bit weird how he was saying this was what led up to my kidnapping. I thought it was all to do with Black Death. Daria continued reading. She could tell I was shocked by what she was saying but it was important to hear everything that was being said. Lukasz told the police he was paid £500,000 but that when he found out they planned to kidnap me, he backed out of the plan. He said he'd needed the money for leukaemia treatment. It was the strangest thing I had heard, and none of it made sense. The reason he gave to the police why he'd kept me at the farmhouse was very different from the Black Death version he had told me, although everything else was similar to my report.

He still claimed that Romanians had drugged me and put me in the car, and he admitted to keeping me at the farmhouse. But no mention of Black Death. I reasoned to myself that he didn't mention Black Death because it would land him in trouble with them. It sort of made sense to me, I guess.

The day I went to court was extremely hot. We walked to the Court of Milan – we, as in myself, Daria and the trainee lawyer. It was about a five-minute walk from Francesco's office and I used the time to try to calm myself down. There was no Nicoletta, which was hard. I was so used to having her around and I missed her greatly. She had been a stranger to me two weeks ago but now she had become such a tower of support. I wasn't sure how I'd got through that previous week without her.

I had been speaking to my mum every couple of hours these past few days. There was nothing she didn't know about what was happening. But Mum would also over-think things. She was more worried now, before court, than ever. What if Black Death had me killed to stop me giving evidence? I couldn't deal with that thought. It was good to talk to her, to hear her voice and get her reassurance, but I still had to face this alone. The courthouse was huge. I couldn't tell you where we went in that building if I tried. I just followed Daria as she made her way around the different floors to the courtroom we would be in.

I was one of the first to enter, as I had asked to sit behind a screen. I didn't want to face Lukasz. I couldn't. It was horrible to think I would even be in the same room as him, but at least this way I knew I couldn't be seen by him. But it wasn't a very good screen. There were three little curtains that had gaps in between them. I could see him.

He didn't come into court until everyone else was seated. I sat behind my curtain screen and there was a microphone in front of me and I had a new interpreter next to me. Then I saw the female judge come in and a man who was on a little computer doing the recording. I also saw Simontacci sitting opposite me across the room. This is OK, I thought. These are the only people I want to see. On the other side of the court were lots of people. Daria, the trainee lawyer, the public prosecutor. There were lots of extra people and police too. And last to walk in was Lukasz. My senses were so acute, I heard the handcuffs first. That was my first clue that the man who had held me captive was coming into the same room as me.

My heart was beating so fast I was convinced he would hear it. I had to try so hard to hold back the tears. I knew if I started to cry that would be it – I wouldn't be able to think straight or talk clearly. I absolutely did not want to see him. But the problem was, when I closed my eyes and told myself I needed to control my breathing and calm myself down, I could see him. So I opened my eyes. And I looked. The curtains weren't doing their job. The gap in between them gave me a clear view of him. There were four armed guards around him. He was sitting diagonal to me on the other side of the room.

The prosecutor asked me to go through everything again – everything I had told the police in my statement. I started to speak but, before I had said more than a few words, the prosecutor asked Lukasz if he could hear me. He said no. So he had to move. He had to move closer to me so he could hear everything that was being said. He moved right next to me, to the other side of the curtain, and now there was just a flimsy piece of cloth between us. I could see him close up now. He had shaved his head and looked very different from how he'd looked at the farmhouse. But he didn't look bothered by anything. He was just sitting there staring into space like he didn't have a care in the world.

The judge asked me to start again. I began to talk but I had to stop after every sentence for the interpreter to relay it to the judge. I tried to speak as clearly as I could into the microphone. I started from Paris. The story didn't make sense without Paris.

I was halfway through telling him what happened when the interpreter started to have a panic attack. She couldn't do it any more, she said. She was crying. To begin with, I didn't have a clue why, and then she said she didn't understand some of the words I was using. She didn't understand when I was explaining about being handcuffed to the 'foot' of the chest of drawers. She started to panic. Apparently there weren't always the Italian words for the English words I was saying. I couldn't believe it. All that went through my mind was that if she stopped, this whole process would have to be postponed and we would all have to start again at a later date. And that would mean I wouldn't be able to go home. I had just started telling the judge about being handcuffed to the chest of drawers when this happened. She couldn't explain it. She didn't know some of the words, like 'auction', and she kept getting it wrong, she said.

She didn't know what to do and was crying and getting very upset about it. Everyone had to leave the court at this point and the prosecutor rang the consulate to try to find another interpreter. But because it was holiday season there were no other interpreters available. No one knew what to do. I just wanted to carry on. I didn't want this to stop, to be postponed and then have to relive it again another day. Eventually, with no other interpreter available, it was decided to continue. It was worked out that I would speak very slowly and I said I would try to find alternative words for her. But that wasn't allowed – the prosecutor was adamant I shouldn't alter anything I said. So I just had to speak really slowly. So we carried on like that but I could see she didn't know some of the words and got all panicked again. I would say something and then she would just look at me, wide-eyed, like she didn't know what to say.

I did try to help her by changing a few words that didn't matter and we got there in the end. Then, when I had finished speaking, the prosecutor addressed me. He wanted me to confirm some statements. He said to me, 'In May this year, did you know Lukasz ordered two black ski masks online?'

He had to ask it as a question rather than a statement and I had to answer. At first he asked me to describe the masks the kidnappers were wearing, so I said they were black and made of wool. They had two eyeholes and a mouth hole. He said to me, 'Were they ski masks?'

And I replied, 'I don't know. I don't know what a ski mask looks like.' It was at that point he told me about Lukasz making that order in May.

I was confused. Why would Lukasz have ordered the masks if he had nothing to do with the kidnapping? If he had no idea about it until the last moment?

'Did you know in June he had ordered a black bag?' The prosecutor's question just hung there. Then he showed me a picture of the policewoman curled up in the bag. The photos are all over the internet; you have probably seen them. A policewoman is curled up in the same bag that had been found at the farmhouse where I was held.

It took my breath away seeing that picture. It took me a

while to work out what I was seeing. I wasn't sure it was my bag, as I had only seen the inside of it. It was just a black, waxy bag to me, so I didn't know. But then I saw the hole. I recognised the hole I had forced my hands through. This was the bag that was found at the house.

Then the bombshell really dropped. I was still trying to process the things he'd said about the ski masks when he said to me, 'Was the person who got into the boot of the car with you Lukasz?'

'No, definitely not,' I said. He asked if I could describe the person. I said, 'Tall, slim build with soft features and short hair. The driver was the same nationality as him.' He wanted to know how I knew that. 'Lukasz told me,' I replied.

And then he told me something that made my blood run cold. He said that the photos of me lying on the studio floor, having just been drugged, were taken on Lukasz's phone. What?! I wanted to scream. That made no sense.

I said, 'How is that possible if Lukasz wasn't at the studio?' How do you know Lukasz wasn't there?

I couldn't make sense of what I was hearing. My brain certainly wasn't joining the pieces together. Lukasz wasn't there; he was the one who saved me…That is what I had believed. Did believe. Used to believe. I just didn't know. It was exhausting. My mind had to hear and relearn everything. Then Simontacci's comments flashed through my mind. I didn't have to worry, he'd said. I guess it made more sense now.

All the time this was going on Lukasz didn't look bothered

in the slightest. It was like he didn't even care. But I didn't understand that either. There was one thing I did feel now. Or didn't, as it were. I didn't feel sorry for him any more. I was still thinking he was the one who'd brought me back, the one who'd saved me from the Romanians. The one who'd saved me from the Romanians who could have killed me. Then, to find out he was one of the masked men? I had no sympathy.

Did Lukasz speak at all? The process was that he could interrupt me at any point in my statement if he heard anything he thought was wrong or untrue. It is why it was so important that he heard everything I said and had to move closer to me. He had to speak through his lawyer, though. And there were two points he wanted me to confirm. He asked his lawyer if I could confirm that he said he was willing to pay some of the ransom, some of the £250,000.

I confirmed he told me that. And then he asked me to confirm that he'd said he would help me get the money to Black Death. I confirmed that. He probably thought these bits of information, confirmed by me, would reduce his sentence. They were silly little points, really, and didn't seem to me to make any sense. Francesco told me later, after he had spoken to his mum and read through the transcript, that Lukasz's lawyer wasn't even trying. He had seen all the evidence against Lukasz and there was no point.

I was in court for an hour or two. It might not even have been that long, in fact, but I felt completely mentally and emotionally drained. The judge said, 'OK,' and everyone just stood up and left. Lukasz went out first. That was it. I was relieved it was over, even though I still had the visit to the house the next day hanging over me.

I left the court and was standing in the corridor with Simontacci, Daria and the trainee lawyer when I saw Lukasz for the last time. He came out of a door with armed guards all around him. He started walking down the hall away from us, and then he looked back at me. It was just a quick glance and then he turned away. That was the last time I saw him.

I left the courthouse feeling completely overwhelmed and confused. I was almost certain he was just a liar. It took a few days to get used to that idea, for that to sink in, but it did. Over the course of the next few days I called my friend Rory. Rory and Phil were telling me the same thing now – they were adamant Lukasz was a fantasist. He *was* a liar. They were trying to get into my head that everything he had previously told me was complete lies.

They were telling me he was just a guy who thought this up with an accomplice and that was it. But it couldn't be, I was thinking. I had seen a bearded man in the front of the car when I first knocked the parcel shelf off. I remembered seeing the side of his face, and there was a beard. They were driving without masks but put them back on to come round to the boot, and Lukasz didn't have a beard, so there must have been another man. I was still scared, even though everything else seemed to show that Lukasz was a liar. It took a while to process it all, as I kept thinking about everything Lukasz had told me while he kept me in the house. Everything I was hearing now seemed the complete opposite of what he'd told me.

I suppose there was an element of reassurance in all this. What I had heard in court, what Simontacci had said, did make me feel a little better. I wasn't completely convinced but I was beginning to accept it was just a guy and his mate, like Rory was trying to tell me. But then, in the back of my mind, there was a third guy. A guy with a beard. So I thought there could have been more people involved.

I spoke to Mum as soon as I got back to the apartment. She was convinced it was still all real, that everything about Black Death was real. She said I couldn't relax, and she didn't want me to be complacent. And she didn't want me to go back to the remote house where I'd been held. Lukasz had told me there were Black Death agents nearby, just down the road from the house. She was convinced I would be taken again if I went there. In my police statement, I had only drawn a picture of the house. Tomorrow I would be identifying it in real life.

CHAPTER 14

Reliving the hell

'You just have to identify everything you see, tell us what is what and then you will be home. It won't take long, Chloe, it won't, I promise.'

I want to tell you that I went to bed after the day at court exhausted but pleased with myself. It was another day done, another thing over with. But I can't. In all honesty, while I was overwhelmingly pleased that I wouldn't ever have to see Lukasz again, that I had done what I needed to do, I still had the house visit hanging over me. It was like a big, dark heaviness that was weighing me down. I was dreading the next day. I was trying to digest things I'd heard in court about Lukasz. I was beginning to see him in a different light, and I could picture an end to him in my life. But that house…that will for ever be etched in my memory. I had kept it shut away and now I had to go back and open that door again, hear those beads rattle again. The house was just bricks and mortar but, to me, it was a living, breathing reminder of my fear. I had to focus on going home, I told myself. My incentive for getting through tomorrow was the thought of going home on Sunday.

★ ★ ★

I set the alarm early for Saturday morning, although I probably slept little that night anyway. As if being worried about visiting the house and the studio again wasn't playing on my mind enough, at midnight I received news that gave me more anxiety. Filippo messaged me and told me that my story was out. It was public news now. I didn't believe him at first but then I remembered the conversation Simontacci had with Carlo earlier that afternoon. He'd said it was only a matter of time and he was right – hardly any time at all! He said the story had broken in one of the biggest newspapers in Italy, *Corriere della Sera*. It was only a matter of hours before everyone else, including the UK media, started reporting on it. I was devastated. I didn't want anyone to know. I wanted to just get done what I needed to do here, go home and put it all behind me. I hadn't been named yet, it just said 'a British model', but I wasn't sure how long that would last. It was another thing to think about on a day I knew I would struggle to get through as it was.

★ ★ ★

I got up at 8am that Saturday as I was due to meet Francesco. He was picking me up from the apartment. It was the first time I had seen him since he had got back from holiday. He collected me from the lobby and we walked to his car and then drove to a nearby petrol station. When we pulled into the petrol station, Simontacci got out of his unmarked police car and came over to see us. He had the interpreter who was in court the previous day with him too, as well as two other police officers. I was pleased there were so many people coming with me. I didn't want it to just be me and one policeman, and I felt safe knowing there were quite a few familiar faces around me.

He explained what was going to happen that day and what I needed to do. I was to be recorded on videotape, for visual evidence of me identifying stuff, and showing the police what had happened to me and where. After the explanation, we got back into Francesco's car and followed the unmarked police car to the studio. We didn't park there; instead we drove and parked on a side road round the corner from the studio. I say 'studio', but of course it wasn't a proper studio. In my mind it was still the place I was meant to go for a photo shoot, but in actual fact it was just an empty building. I didn't know why we didn't park in front of the building until Francesco explained that a police press conference was scheduled for that morning. The press would be keen to hear all the details from the police, which meant that journalists would be making their own investigations and getting their own photos. Simontacci wanted to make sure there were no journalists outside the studio, so we walked over to it, ready to turn back if so.

When we got out of the car we had to put on forensics

gloves. It was a crime scene still and, although the forensics team had done what they needed to do, we weren't allowed to touch anything. We stopped right outside the building and I noticed, across the street, another police car. It had two armed guards in it as well. I can't tell you how reassuring that was, having so many people there with me. They stayed in the car, they didn't follow us into the building, but I knew they were there.

Simontacci motioned that they were ready to start recording, and he spoke first, saying the date and our location for the video.

The interpreter was told she had to repeat on camera what I was saying after every few words. We started at the place I had got out of the taxi. The camera followed me when I walked to the bigger building, the number 7 building. I explained as clearly as I could everything I did that day. The door was locked, I said, so I called the number that was on the email. I was trying to be clear so the video would pick up what I was saying and the interpreter could keep up. I explained the conversation I had with the man on the phone who told me to just walk in but I said I couldn't because it was locked. And then they followed me as I walked round the corner and found the little building. This was the building I had entered, I said, and that is where I walked in, guided by the man on the phone.

My heart skipped a little at that point.

It was really strange, as I was doing this, as I was talking through what I had done only a few weeks previously. I was looking around at everything. I was taking everything in. The first time I had been here I was just living it and wasn't paying attention to what was going on, or what things looked like in any great detail. But now I was. We went into the studio and I saw those black boards again, positioned to lead me to a particular place in the building. Seeing them now, I just thought, Oh my God. They looked so tacky. I was seeing it through eyes that were wary; eyes that now knew what had gone on here. This place wasn't frightening to me, though; it didn't have a hold on me. I had probably been in there for only a few minutes before I was drugged. And then, well, I don't know how long I was in there unconscious but that didn't affect me. It had all happened so quickly. I didn't have any sort of emotional attachment with the place. I had to confirm on tape the spot where I was standing when I was grabbed from behind, and I had to show them how I was physically restrained. I also had to confirm that I didn't go in either the room that had the word 'studio' on it or the room at the end of the corridor. The sign was no longer there. It was one of the things I noticed straight away. Lukasz had obviously put up a temporary sign to keep everything seemingly normal for me.

★ ★ ★

The forensics team had removed all my clothes from the studio when they first investigated, so there wasn't anything else to do. We probably weren't in there much longer today than I had been on the day of the kidnap.

I felt good after that. The list for today was the studio, the village and then the house – and I had already done the studio. It was one off the list. I wasn't looking forward to the next two but I had to focus and just get them over with. The studio had no strong emotional hold over me but I knew the emotions of the rest of the day might not be so easily overcome.

The armed police in the stationary car stayed where they were as we left the studio. I got back into Francesco's car, while Simontacci, the interpreter and the two other police officers went in Simontacci's car. We travelled in convoy to the village and we stayed behind his car the whole way. I knew we were in for a long drive, and I was grateful that we stopped at a service station on the way to break up the journey. We all got out to get a drink and stretch our legs. It was a very hot day, a beautiful Italian summer's day, but I didn't see it like that. It should have been dark and overcast and cold, I thought – that suited the day we had planned much more than glorious sunshine.

Simontacci came over to our car and told Francesco that the DA had officially released my passport. I was so happy. It was official. I couldn't believe it – I would actually be going home tomorrow. It was such a great motivation to get this day over with. Francesco told me that after all this was over he would take me to the police station to get my passport. Now I had something to look forward to.

After about three and a half hours, we drove into the village. We parked in a car park on the outskirts of the village, where another car was waiting for us containing two forensics officers from Turin who were joining our convoy.

Simontacci explained what I had to do now. I was to get

into the front passenger seat of the forensics team's car while he and the interpreter sat in the back. They would film me from behind and I would have to identify on the camera everything I had mentioned in my statement – the fruit shop, the shoe shop, the car park. So I did. I got into the passenger seat and one of the police officers drove us through the village. They were all waiting for me to say what bits I recognised and identify the shops, but we drove all the way through the village and came out the other end and I didn't recognise anything! The thing was, when Lukasz took me to the village we had come in from the other end. We were coming from the Turin end, not the way in from Milan.

So I said, 'Can we turn round and try it from this way, as this is the way I came in before?' I was hoping that doing it the right way, the route Lukasz had taken me into the village, would make more sense. And so we did. We turned round and drove on – and I recognised it all straight away. I remember seeing the grocery store as soon as we came in. It had a stripy roof that I recognised. And then there was the little car park, the one Lukasz parked in. I identified it and we pulled in there.

We parked the car and all got out. From there, I then had to walk down the windy road and show them the route we took to the shop. They were following me the whole time with the camera. We walked down the street, I pointed out the grocery store again, and then tried to concentrate on finding the shoe shop. When I had come with Lukasz, I was just following him. I wasn't paying much attention to how many other shops there were or what was going on. It was only now that I realised how many shoe shops there were on the street! They all looked the same from the outside. I knew I would recognise the one we had gone in from the inside but I couldn't by just looking at the exterior.

All the doors were open as we went past, so I could clearly see inside. I was still being recorded and I knew I would be able to recognise the right one if I could see the inside. And I did. I found the shop. We didn't go in but I could see in well enough to know it was the right one. I then led them back to the little car park and we all got in the car and drove back to the bigger car park where Francesco and the others were waiting for us.

Another bit done, I thought to myself, as I got out of the forensics team's car. But instead of everyone getting back into their cars again, they started milling around and chatting. We were waiting in the car park for something but I didn't know why. I saw that the forensics guys had gone, so perhaps we were waiting for them to return. Francesco was doing something in his car and the others were just standing, hanging around. I didn't want to be waiting here. I just wanted to go, to leave this place. I was stressing out. 'Why can't we just go?' I wanted to scream at them but, instead, screamed it in my head. All these horrible thoughts started running through my mind and I turned away from the group and began to move away from them. I started to cry. I had the safety of the police and everyone around me and yet I was petrified. It was the thought of being back in the area where I was held…it was too much.

It was the interpreter who spotted me first and she came over to see if I was OK. She didn't really know what to say to me or how to comfort me, but then I saw Francesco look around and spot me. He came right over and led me to his car. I told him I didn't want to hang around here any more, I just wanted to get this all over with. I still had the thought of the house to do after this, the next and final stage. I sat there in the front seat of his car crying. Either he said something or Simontacci realised what was going on, as all of a sudden we were on the move again.

The cars seemed to speed up after that. There were three cars in the convoy now, following us to the house. We were behind Simontacci again. Francesco was trying to comfort and reassure me; he wanted to make sure I was OK. I was still crying but I was trying to mentally prepare myself for the house visit that I knew was only a few minutes' drive away now.

'It will be quick,' he said. 'You just have to identify everything you see, tell us what is what and then you will be home. It won't take long, Chloe, it won't, I promise.' And then he said something to me that I'll never forget. He said, 'Chloe, you have to remember this: nothing will ever feel like a challenge for you now after going through this.'

Nothing that life throws at me will ever compare to the ordeal that I have endured and survived. Not many people will understand it. People will sympathise but no one will 'get' it. And what he said is so true. All the stuff in the media, all the crap I have had from people, all the messages of hate, the interviewers who have basically accused me of lying or misleading everyone. It's water off a duck's back. Francesco's 'challenge' comment has stuck with me and surviving this has made me a stronger person.

We continued in the convoy of cars travelling on the road to the house. I knew it wouldn't be long until we got there and, sure enough, Francesco saw Simontacci stop at the bottom of the windy road the house was on, and slowed down and stopped our car. Simontacci got out of his car and came round to where we had parked. But I wasn't ready. I was crying and I didn't think at this point I would be able to move out of Francesco's car.

'Give us a minute,' Francesco told Simontacci, and he nodded and moved away. I knew this would be hard. I had psyched myself up for this and now it was time to get it over with. I had to stay there for a few minutes to compose myself. I knew I had to get myself together. Crying wasn't going to help. I was safe. I just needed to get this done and that was it. I got out of Francesco's car and got into the forensics car again. I was in the front passenger seat and Simontacci and the interpreter were in the back and videoing from there again.

We had to drive up the road, past the row of houses and all the ruins, and I had to identify the house where I was held prisoner. I will never forget that house. I had to point it out, physically point for the videotape, and I did – we drove past the white house and I confirmed that was the right one.

The car stopped and we all got out. We put on forensic gloves again and Simontacci warned us all again not to touch anything. I turned to face the direction of the house. It was time to walk up the hill. The others followed me and I led the way while the filming carried on from behind. I focused on my feet, one foot in front of the other, step by step. I was going to do this but I was going to do it quickly and get it over with.

Simontacci went in front to open the door. Then we were in the kitchen. I knew we were filming and I knew they were waiting for me to speak, so I did. I pointed to a bit of the kitchen floor and said, 'This is where I got out of the bag.' That was it. Nothing else to say. Then I led them upstairs. I pointed to a room on the left and confirmed I had never entered. Then I took them into the first room. Those beads...that noise...I stopped when I went in. I pointed to the the chest of drawers and said, 'This is where I was handcuffed,' and showed them which foot of the chest of drawers my hands had been handcuffed to, and the end to which my feet had been fastened. I pointed at the floor, showing them where my sleeping bag had been positioned.

My interpreter was repeating everything I said straight after I said it. She knew I didn't need to say much. I was just trying to force myself to speak, say what I needed to say and then go. I showed them the bathroom and the shower and then took them into the double bedroom. I didn't need to go right in; I didn't need to lie on the bed any more and be told there was an auction for my life happening in a matter of days, or that Black Death were watching my every move. I nodded to the double bed. I could hear myself speak but I didn't think it was coming from me. It was like I was hearing someone else say it.

'That's the side of the bed I slept on. The red blanket was

mine, the yellow one was Lukasz's,' I said. My blanket was now screwed up in a ball on the floor. And that was it.

All the forensics testing had been done those past three weeks. I wasn't going to touch anything but I knew what they had found here: his semen on the bed. My hair on the bed. That was the science, the black and whiteness of it, but the emotion of being held there, they couldn't see or test or measure for that.

I just wanted to get out now. I was done. I had turned myself into a machine for this but I was aware that my resolve was weakening.

I didn't want to cry on videotape and in front of everyone. Francesco had said to me in the car that if I cried I would have to repeat myself for the tape as it might not pick up everything I said. It wouldn't be clear and they needed to clearly hear what I was identifying and, if not, the whole process would take longer. I didn't want to be here longer than I needed to be. I went out of the bedroom and back down the stairs. I remembered that day of leaving, that early start nearly three weeks before. I thought then that I would be leaving for the last time – now I was definite I would be.

We got out into the front garden area and I heard someone shut the door behind us. That slam noise, that definite close. It was such a relief. I was closing the door on that part of my life now. I was safe. I had to remember that: I was safe. I had survived. I had my life to lead now. And actually, I told myself, this house wasn't going to have a hold on me any more. I wasn't going to let it.

We all walked back down to the car in silence but when

we got there everyone started talking to me. They were all really pleased. They told me I had done well and were congratulating me. The police and Francesco and Simontacci asked if I wanted to have dinner with them all, to celebrate that I was going home tomorrow. It was all over. And it was such a relief, but I still didn't want to hang around. I didn't want to stay there any longer than I needed to. So I moved quickly to Francesco and back into the safety of his car.

I agreed to go to dinner. Everyone else was going and it seemed a good way to finish the day. We drove back to the village and found this little restaurant. It was the same village we had been to not more than a couple of hours earlier but it felt like a different place. I was done with this now; I had done what I needed to do. We could all go and eat.

We sat round a big table and everyone was celebrating and toasting me: 'For Chloe!' they said. We all ate a pasta dish but I'm not sure what it was. I was really proud of myself – I guess I thought by the way they were celebrating that I had done all they had asked of me. I had helped them prevent this happening to others, they told me. They were all drinking beer and I had an orange juice. We ate and spent about an hour there. It wasn't a big thing but, in some respects, it was a massive occasion.

It was while we were in the restaurant that we realised the UK media had now got hold of the story. Francesco had been alerted and told me first, but it wasn't long before I was getting calls from Phil and Rory. They told me it was everywhere, all over the news, the internet. I still hadn't been named for my own safety, as I was still in Italy. Both

Rory and Phil were quite positive about it. It was good, they said; it was a good story because it had a happy ending and I might be able to help others like me. I honestly couldn't think about that right now.

The Italian police had given a press conference that morning and it was worldwide news in a matter of hours. I borrowed Francesco's phone at the dinner table and read through what the media were reporting. It was very strange – I was reading a story about me, about what had happened to me, and yet I felt very distant from it. The *Mail Online* had the most coverage and a video of the police answering questions at the press conference. Milan Deputy Prosecutor Paolo Storari was videoed saying this about Lukasz: 'Fantasist or not, what is clear is that he is a very dangerous man who drugged his victim as soon as she was kidnapped and put her inside a large travel bag in the boot of a car. His version of events is barely credible but clearly he does not deny that he was with her for the time she was missing.'

Filippo was right – the *Corriere della Sera* was quoted as reporting the story first. But it wasn't just Italian and British media. American news sites like CNN, *USA Today*, *Washington Post* and Fox News were reporting my kidnapping, as well as websites in Australia like news.com.au and 9.news.com and Middle Eastern websites like Arab News.

They were all reporting the highlights from the police press conference. A police official, Lorenzo Bucossi, had told the Italian journalists that: 'Attacked, drugged, handcuffed and closed inside a suitcase, that's how a twenty-year-old

English model was kidnapped on July 11 in Milan to be sold to the best offer on pornography sites on the internet. The kidnappers loaded the suitcase with the girl inside into a car trunk and drove to a rural home in a hamlet outside Turin'.

I could see why everyone wanted to know about the story, why there was such a huge interest in it, but to everyone else – to those reporting it, to those reading it – it was just a story. It had happened to me. Me alone.

CHAPTER 15

Going home

'To the police, not only had I survived but I had allowed them to catch the guy who potentially could have kidnapped other girls. Maybe their own daughters. It could have happened to them and I think they saw me and the conclusion to this case as a miracle.'

After dinner Francesco drove me back to the police station to get my passport. I had to go into a room and sign for it before I was allowed it back and it was so amazing to get it. I was allowed to have only my passport and my driving licence returned to me; the police kept everything else. So I signed more forms that allowed Francesco to collect my other belongings, like my phone and my purse and clothes, when they were ready to be released. I didn't care too much about the other bits. I had my passport; that was all I cared about. I expected to go straight back to my apartment after that but there were lots of police officials who wanted to come and say goodbye to me. I ended up chatting to quite a few of them in the corridor. No one mentioned Lukasz and I didn't ask about him – I didn't care about him now or what was going to happen to him. He wasn't my saviour. He wasn't the one who had come to rescue me. He didn't mean anything to me now.

Simontacci took me to the investigation room and showed me a picture of his daughter. He had shown me lots of photos of her over dinner too. He told me she wanted to live in London when she was older. He said that she was his motivation for working twenty hours a day on this case. He had imagined what it would be like if I was his daughter. If she had been me. She was slightly younger than me, I think he said a couple of years, but it was too close to home for him.

I gave Simontacci a hug and thanked him for everything he had done and then I said goodbye. I went out to find Francesco, who was on the phone. It was the head of the police, he said. She wanted to thank me for everything. She had a daughter as well, she told Francesco. It seemed lots of them had daughters who were my age or younger, and they all felt an emotional connection. To the police, not only had I survived but I had allowed them to catch the guy who potentially could have kidnapped other girls. Maybe their own daughters. It could have happened to them, and I think they saw me and the conclusion to this case as a miracle.

It was time to go back to the apartment. I had a lot of packing to do. I had spoken to my mum a lot that day; she knew everything that was happening and she knew I was safe. I told her I had my passport back and I would see her tomorrow. It was so amazing to be able to say that!

Francesco drove me back to the apartment and we hugged and said goodbye. I was so grateful for everything he had done and how he had helped me – not just with the legal side of things but with all the emotional support too. Then, as I went into the lobby, the first person I saw waiting for me was Carlo. We started talking and he wanted to order us some food for that evening, so he did. It wasn't like I hadn't eaten recently but I was happy to sit and eat again with Carlo. He had helped me a lot too. When the food arrived we ate it together in a room behind the reception desk. I will always remember his face the first night I turned up with just a plastic bag containing a few clothes and no ID! I won't forget the kindness he and Filippo showed me.

Carlo knew the story was out in the press. He asked if I wanted to use his laptop, so I did. I sat eating takeaway and started reading about how the world was reporting my story. I logged on to my Facebook page and the first thing I saw was that one of my friends had shared the article in the news feed. I couldn't switch off from it. It was so weird looking at Facebook, so weird! My life was completely different from the last time I had been on it; it was like a world away. My world had changed beyond recognition and yet here were my friends, posting away about all the normal stuff.

I closed the laptop. It was time to go up to my room and start packing. I said goodbye to Carlo, gave him a big hug and thanked him. I was going to the airport early in the morning, so I knew he wouldn't be around to say goodbye then – he would be fast asleep!

That evening, while I was packing, my phone rang. It was a lady from the consulate. She wanted to brief me on what was going to happen the following day when I got to the airport. She told me I wouldn't be able to go through the main Arrivals when I landed at Gatwick. I would have to get picked up from a separate area in case there was too much media interest at the main gate. I would have to give her the names of the people who were going to collect me, as they would need to go to a special VIP lounge where I would wait for them. At that point I didn't know who was going to come – I didn't know if it would be Rory, Danielle or Phil. I said I would let her know. I know Phil wanted to come – they all wanted to come. Danielle and Rory don't know each other but they both hate Phil, so I knew Phil wouldn't be keen on going with them both there. I didn't want Phil to come anyway. At the time I felt he was the cause of all this. I blamed him for everything

The lady from the consulate also wanted to explain to me that my name would eventually come out. She told me it wouldn't be released by them but it was inevitable that I would be identified. She was just warning me to delete stuff from my social media, stuff that I didn't want anyone seeing as, sooner or later, the press and journalists would be looking into everything and seeing everything. To be honest, as she was saying this, I didn't really know what it meant. I certainly didn't know what it would mean for my life – photographers outside my house, people wanting to talk to me all the time about what happened. It was good of her to say something but I didn't appreciate the impact of this media intrusion at that point. My head was solely focused on getting home. I finished packing my luggage and spent my last night in Italy.

The police had arranged a car to pick me up at 8am the following morning. The policeman waiting for me in the car was one I recognised from the previous day. It wasn't just him though, there were two other police officers in the car too. Three policemen and me – I couldn't be in safer hands, I thought.

We drove to Linate Airport in Milan, and during the car ride Serena, the woman police detective who interviewed me with Simontacci on the first day, called and asked to speak to me. I hadn't had chance to say goodbye to her the day before and I was pleased when the phone was passed to me so I could speak to her. She was very sweet. She had just called to wish me a great life, she said.

We arrived at the airport and were met by an airport police guy who took us upstairs. We didn't have to do the usual customs clearance or check-in or anything but went straight through the security section and ended up waiting in a room. Then, eventually, it was time to go. I got taken down to a police car that was outside the building, where all the planes were parked or taxiing. It was pouring with rain but it wasn't cold. I wondered if it would be raining in England, whether it was typical British summer weather or not. I would soon find out. We waited in the car for ages, it seemed, but then we saw the plane arrive. I was going to be the first passenger on it, before everyone else, so the policeman I recognised previously got out of the car with me and escorted me onto the plane.

I thought he might leave me at the bottom of the flight of stairs but he boarded the plane with me and took me to my seat. The flight staff were aware of what had happened and they were very kind. They said to let them know if I needed anything. The policeman then said goodbye and that was it. No more Italian police escort, just me, a person on a flight to the UK. All the other passengers got on the plane like they didn't have a care in the world. And why would they? They were holidaymakers. Relatives visiting families. People on business trips. And me... I couldn't exactly share the same stories, could I? The plane was ready for take-off and it would be only a matter of moments before we were airborne. I was going home. It was real. It was a normal flight, but in so many other ways it was not normal. I closed my eyes and waited for the judder of take-off.

★ ★ ★

The plane bumped and jolted a little as we landed at Gatwick and I wanted to jump right out of my seat. We were here. Back in the UK. Back home. We were all disembarking at the same time, so I had to wait while everyone else gathered up their bags and started to queue in the aisle. It felt like it was taking for ever, but then, that stage always does, and in that regard I was no different from anyone else. Everyone wanted to get off the plane and go back to their homes or their loved ones. When I got to the door, the cabin crew told me to make my way to the officers in hi-vis jackets at the bottom of the steps.

So I did just that and they led me to a car waiting nearby. While everyone else was headed for the main bit of the airport, they told me they were taking me to the Sussex Suite, an area specifically reserved for VIP guests and arrivals.

It was Rory who was coming to collect me but he wasn't there when we entered the suite. He was having problems getting there, as it was such a hard place to find apparently. Eventually he arrived. I hadn't seen him for ages – we weren't speaking before I had left for Milan, as we'd had a trivial argument back in April time. But I had told Lukasz he was someone who might be able to help me; he was one of the three on my list. I had been speaking to Rory as soon as I had been given the mobile phone by the police. We'd been going over all the new information I was hearing about Lukasz. He was helping me piece bits of the puzzle together. As soon as he came through the door I gave him a big hug. It was emotional and, of course, I was pleased to see him but I wanted to get home now.

I rang Mum and told her I was on my way home, as I had promised her I would. She wanted to check that Rory had met me but when I spoke to her she warned me there was lots of press outside the house.

Rory wasn't fazed; we would just go round the back, he said. When we got to my house we did exactly that. I walked through the back gate and it felt like I had been away a matter of hours rather than weeks. Everything was the same; nothing had changed. I saw my dog. I called her name and she looked back at me and just froze. My dog was just staring at me. I could see her tail wagging but she wasn't sure... It felt like she was looking at me for ages before she came bounding over. It was so nice to see her. I bent down and gave her the biggest cuddle, nestling my head in her soft fur and breathing in her wonderful smell. My Nylah, I have missed you! I thought. There was no sign of my mum at this point. The back door was unlocked but she wasn't in. Typical! I knew she hadn't gone far and it was only a matter of minutes before I heard the front door open.

Have you ever not seen someone for ages and you picture them in your mind and then, when you see them, you think, Oh yes, you haven't really been away from me at all because I've seen you every day in my mind? It was like I had said goodbye to her only the previous day, not nearly four weeks ago. It was like nothing had happened at all. But she was crying and we were hugging and it felt so good to cuddle her.

The reality was, however, that journalists and paparazzi were outside the house and had been outside for hours, Mum said. Phil wouldn't stop ringing my mobile. I knew the press wouldn't leave me alone now, and Rory was saying I had to go outside and see them otherwise they wouldn't go away. It was the absolute last thing I wanted to do after the past couple of days of confronting everything that happened. I just wanted to stay in the house, curl up under my lovely warm duvet, sleep in my bed, see my son, walk my dog and forget about all of this. I didn't know what to say to the press – where on earth would I begin?! I didn't want to say anything, but Rory was right. The sooner I confronted them, said my bit, the sooner they would go and then I could relax.

He would write something for me to say, he said. So we prepared a little script together. I was still in the clothes I had worn on the flight home. I had probably been home less than an hour and I was now going to go out and show myself to the world. But then they would leave me alone, I thought, so it would be worth it. So I did it. I went out, on my own, to face the press. Well, Nylah was with me. I spoke the lines we had written and that was it. They wanted to ask me more questions; they wanted to know more, but I said I wasn't going to say anything more. I did what I did that morning to get some peace, to be left alone.

★ ★ ★

That evening, me and Mum went on a dog walk together. It was the most amazing feeling, doing this simple, normal thing – just walking the dog together. I had wished I could do this simple act when I was in Italy. Mum and I didn't need to talk. We had talked every day since I'd been given that phone. We spoke at least seven times a day, so it didn't feel like I hadn't seen her for over three weeks. There wasn't anything to say; we had conversationed out! We just wanted to be together and it was so nice to walk next to her. The silence spoke volumes: we were together; I was home.

★ ★ ★

A lot of people criticised me for not showing more emotion in that interview outside my house – to break down, to cry, to show myself to be more of a 'victim'. I hope you can see the true picture of that encounter now – that for three weeks I had been living as a victim, and now I wasn't a victim any more. I was finally free. I was home and I was safe. I had such criticism over what I was wearing, too. 'She doesn't dress like she has just been kidnapped,' people said. I had just taken a flight from a hot country in the height of summer and I didn't have an extensive wardrobe! I didn't change for the cameras. I wore exactly what I flew back in. What was I supposed to wear?

But that isn't to say I didn't feel completely and utterly overwhelmed when I flew back to the UK. Of course I did. I was in a bit of a daze. I did not want this story to come out. I was mortified. I was embarrassed. I just wanted to forget everything. And I am not media trained either – something else I think people forget. I wasn't scared going out to face reporters but, at the same time, I hadn't done anything like that before in my life. So yes, it was a little bit daunting. I spoke how I always speak; there was no fake act, no 'put-on' tears for the camera. I could be matter-of-fact now because, well, because I was home. I have repeated my story so many times to so many different people – the consulate, the police, the lawyers, the judge, Phil, my mum. I can withdraw myself from it now. Which, if you think about, is a method of survival, isn't it? Distancing yourself from an event helps you deal with it. And I have lived it. So I think I am entitled to do whatever I need to do to deal with it.

CHAPTER 16

Behind the headlines

*'I wasn't worried about speaking with Piers. I knew he
would give me a hard time but, in a way, it just showed
I had nothing to hide when I answered him back every time.
I stood up to him and told him everything he needed
to know. I didn't have anything to be ashamed of. I was
happy to answer everything he asked.'*

Things moved quite quickly for me that first week back. I
tried to switch off from it all but I was being reminded of my
'story' constantly. In terms of how the investigation into my
kidnapping was going, I was finished with the Italian police. I
wouldn't need to liaise with them again, but they did tell me
that the British police would be in touch. I knew of some of
them. I had spoken to one officer, called Drew, when I was
in Milan. He was based in Lincolnshire, where Phil lived.
Phil had contacted the police there when he knew I'd been

kidnapped. Drew had spoken to me several times and he was a reassuring voice. He said he was trying his hardest to get me home, as he believed I could do everything I needed to do via video link. Then there were the two police officers who'd looked after my mum, Mark and Erin. I met them when I returned home.

So what happened now I was home? It was a bit of a whirlwind really. I didn't read anything that was written about me that week. Well, I did at first, and then I quickly realised it was hateful and full of doubt and accusations. I didn't want to read any more. But I knew I had to get my story across now that it was so public. I had come to terms with that. No, I never wanted the story to come out in the first place, but yes, I was ready to tell my side of it now. If the details were out, then I wanted to be the one to tell everyone exactly what had happened.

My first deal was with the *Mail on Sunday*. I signed that deal on the Monday. Phil had been calling me constantly on Sunday when I got back. He left me so many messages but I didn't want to talk to him. All of his messages were about how many emails he had been getting, and all the offers that had been coming in for me. I had been back only a few hours and I couldn't care less. I didn't answer his calls. I couldn't deal with it. He was pressuring me to speak to him but it was because he wanted me to sign deals and agree to contracts. I spoke to him once and said I would speak to him another time. That time came the next day, on the Monday. Rory had introduced me to Mark, the owner of the Kruger Cowne agency.

I spoke to Mark on the phone on Sunday and arranged to go to his offices on Monday. He told me not to say anything to anyone and he arranged for a Virgin motorbike to collect me on Monday morning. We had a meeting at his office, everyone who worked for him and Rory and me. I agreed to sign a twelve-month contract to work with him. And it was while I was in that meeting that Phil called me again. I showed Mark the caller ID and he answered the phone on my behalf. Mark didn't give Phil much time to speak – he completely shut him down. He told him that I would not be working with him again, that I had signed a new contract and that there was no need to contact me again. That was the last I heard of Phil, although I saw him on *Good Morning Britain*, a few weeks later.

After I signed with Mark, my deal with the *Mail on Sunday* was agreed. But because they had my exclusive story, and didn't want anyone else to feature pictures of me or talk to me before it came out the following Sunday, part of my contract was that I couldn't stay at my house. So, having arrived back in the UK on Sunday, and signed the deal with Mark on Monday, and then the *Mail on Sunday* on Tuesday, I found myself staying in a hotel from Tuesday night onwards. I had just got home and I was staying away again. The *Mail on Sunday* appreciated how hard this was for me and said someone could stay with me if I wanted. I called my friend Danielle and she agreed. It would be from Tuesday night until Saturday night and, in that time, I wasn't allowed to talk to anyone or say anything.

It was during this week that other papers started to get

nasty about me. I think they needed a new way of covering my story, and that meant questioning what had happened. On social media some people were posting photos of themselves trying to hide in a luggage bag. What sort of people would make fun of someone who had been kidnapped? How can that be right? Shame on them.

But probably the most hurtful and annoying thing was, that first week everyone was being so nasty I had to be quiet and not respond to any of these allegations. And no one knew why. I wasn't allowed to say anything because of the contract. It was good to finally have my say and tell in detail everything that happened. We went through it day by day. It helped me to explain to everyone exactly what had happened.

Once my story had come out on the Sunday, straight from my mouth, as it were, I did some interviews. The first one on the Monday was on *This Morning*. On Monday I wasn't nervous at all. I don't get nervous. I knew what I had to say. I knew all there was to say. The only thing I had to remember was to pretend the cameras weren't there. Ruth Langsford and Eamonn Holmes were so kind and welcoming when I first arrived. And during the interview I did forget we were in a television studio, and I did get upset. I think I was naïve to think I wouldn't when it came to talking about it, although it has got easier with time. Eamonn was very protective and sympathetic when he was reading out the comments afterwards. I also always had Mark from the agency with me – he accompanied me to all the interviews and stayed the whole time. It was reassuring. He told me if anyone said anything inappropriate, or about my private life, he would just take me off the show. He made that clear to everyone before I filmed anything, so everyone knew where they stood. That was the difference between Mark and Phil. Mark cared. He understood the importance of having someone with me, travelling with me to different countries for shoots, as well as being there for interviews.

After *This Morning*, my next TV interview was on *Lorraine* with Christine Lampard. She was also very welcoming. That was a fairly quick interview but she wanted to cover things I hadn't said on *This Morning*. Christine wanted to know what sort of things I wanted to do next, what the future held for me. We talked about a book. This book idea had come about quite early on after signing with Mark. I had no deal at the time of speaking to Christine but I liked the idea. I liked the idea of being able to tell everything, all the details, all the things that happened to me, so people didn't need to speculate or question things any more. And the thing is, I was beginning to feel comfortable talking about it – I was being offered so many interviews with American TV, Australian TV, so why not? Rory said to me that the more public I am, the safer I am. That is how it came about that I did so many interviews in the first place. No one is going to touch me when everything I was doing was being reported in the media.

★ ★ ★

My interview with Piers Morgan on *Good Morning Britain* was different. I was expecting it to be. There was so much stuff in the papers and online, that interest in my story was rife again. Of course, the bit the papers loved was the shoe-shopping trip. They even made it sound like I was shopping for designer shoes in central Milan. My 'shoe-shopping trip with my captor', like we sauntered around the shops for ages until I found a pretty pair of expensive shoes that I liked, when in fact it was a pair of trainers from a village shop. Pathetic.

So I wasn't worried about speaking with Piers. I knew he would give me a hard time but, in a way, it just meant I had nothing to hide when I answered him back every time. I stood up to him and told him everything he needed to know. I didn't have anything to hide. I like the confrontation with people if they think they know me, or think they know the truth, and I was happy to answer anything he asked me.

I did get a certain idea about TV presenters though. I had met Eamonn and Ruth before my interview, and Christine Lampard, and there was time to say hello and to chat in the studio before I went on air, but I hadn't met Piers Morgan or Dr Phil, the American TV host, before I recorded their shows. Speaks volumes for the sort of interview I would have depending on if I'd met the host or not.

Francesco kept me up to date with things in Italy but I didn't want to go to any court hearing or make any statements outside the court. The police could deal with all of that. I didn't need to have anything to do with it. I had done my bit. I couldn't put my life on hold while I waited to see what happened to Lukasz. I planned to get on with my life.

I find it funny how people question me about Lukasz's tactics. Like I'm meant to know why he did certain things, or acted in certain ways. So, risking repeating myself, I just want to say I HAVE NO IDEA! I don't know why he did what he did. He is completely insane. I DON'T KNOW why he took me to the consulate. I DON'T KNOW why he would go to the effort of drugging and kidnapping me. I DON'T KNOW why he took me into the village for shoes.

But I DO KNOW that it is hard to understand. For me to understand. What started off as Black Death transpired to being just him and his accomplice. The hundreds of agents who he said would be watching me and would kill me if I tried to escape didn't exist. He pretended not to be the masked man but he was. What was to stop him killing me like he said he would if I didn't obey the rules? Who else would do it? It was just him! So yes, it's so confusing. I feel like I am only really understanding it now, and I have had help from the police and investigators. If I was still thinking the things I was thinking when I was being held captive, and for the majority of those three weeks in Milan – that Black Death were after me – I would be a mess.

All the media headlines are carefully edited to favour a man who is guilty of my kidnapping. 'Model helped write her own ransom note' was one I remember reading. Not, '"Model helped write her own ransom note," says man on trial accused of her kidnapping'. People who just read the headlines read that one sentence about me and made up their minds.

The media have helped uncover some of the lies Lukasz

told me. Like the one about him never visiting the UK. I think it was the *Sun* who did an interview with his boss from a recruitment agency where Lukasz worked. He got a job working for DHL, as a delivery driver in Birmingham, but then kept taking unexplained time off.

His boss had apparently called him 'a pathological liar', as he had made up stories about having leukaemia, and that he had to visit his doctor in London. And then there was an ex-girlfriend who told the papers she thought he was a respectable businessman. Lukasz had apparently told her he was in America meeting new clients – at the same time he was holding me in Italy!

But all the investigations, all the things that have come out about him lying...the main thing is I don't need to be afraid of some huge criminal organisation. And I don't need to worry about what people think of me. I am safe.

CHAPTER 17

Notes from my lawyer

*'Doubt is great. Doubting and questioning things is cool,
it's a very intelligent thing to do. But doubt must always
be balanced or measured in front of reality and in
front of evidence.'*

Before this all comes to an end, I want you to hear from
my lawyer, Francesco Pesce. I want you to know exactly
what he thought of my case, his thoughts on Lukasz and the
whole investigation, written before the verdict. Here he is:

FRANCESCO PESCE, CRIMINAL LAWYER.
I remember the day I met Chloe. It was me and two people
here in the office, and we were working on things to do
before the summer. It was a quiet and lazy day that day and
then we received a phone call from the British Consulate.
We are on their list of English-speaking criminal lawyers,

and those are quite rare in Italy. So they called us and this lady, Nicoletta, she was quite agitated on the phone and she told me she had an issue. 'Can we come to your office?' she asked. Of course, I said, and they came. She arrived with Chloe. And Chloe told me her story from the beginning. It was an incredible story.

In those few days in mid-July, Chloe came back and forth to my office quite a lot – more or less every day. She was in her hotel room and she didn't want to stay there too much. She was scared, she didn't know what was happening, and I had people go and get her and take her back and forth so she wasn't ever left alone.

She came to my office once with Ms McDougall, the UK consul from Rome. She had come to Milan for the same purpose. It was a very delicate thing, Chloe's situation. The issue with the consulate was that the DA's office wasn't giving back Chloe's documents because they needed her for the investigation hearing. Some MPs from London started to press issues against our system, wondering why she wasn't back in the UK yet. She was on the list of missing people; they knew she was safe at the consulate, and that was the best part of it, but she couldn't leave Italy for a couple of weeks.

Chloe was quite scared about this because she had no idea why. The consulate, whose main objective is to ensure the wellbeing of their British citizens, was very worried about the whole thing. Why isn't the DA letting Chloe go back?

So they asked me to go to the DA to find a deal. I went to Dr Ilda Boccassini's office the next morning. She is a famous

DA and a very kind woman. She and Dr Paolo Storari were the two DAs proceeding against [Lukasz] Herba. I asked her what could be done there and then, to help Chloe get home. I understood that they still needed her. And she promised me, she gave me her word that they would work as quickly as they could and then they would give Chloe's passport back and let her return to her family. The consulate wanted this in writing, but the DA couldn't do that: that was against every kind of procedure. It was a very delicate thing. The consulate even wanted to give Chloe special permission to leave without her passport but certainly her name would have been on the 'special people' list at the airport and they would have blocked her at Customs. That would have caused a huge incident between Italy and the UK and they were terrified – they didn't want to create a mess out of another mess. So I was the liaison between the DA's office in Italy and the whole British government. We followed Chloe's case day by day.

★ ★ ★

She came to my office and I told her what was happening. And then we had the hearing on 4 August. It was a court hearing, a deposition in front of a judge and then a cross-examination from Mr Herba's lawyer. She requested a curtain between her and Mr Herba and I knew she was scared. The trial hadn't started yet; there are procedures here in Italy that allow you to anticipate part of a hearing – the classic example would be in a case of sexual abuse against children. You are not going to hear from them in a trial – you wouldn't put them through that; it's too delicate – so you can request this type of hearing. It means they will be listened to in front of a judge and the DA and the defendant's lawyer, so it is as if the trial has already started. So this was done for Chloe, in order for her to avoid coming back to Italy. My mother went with her to court, as I had to travel abroad, but I had explained the case fully to my mother. She is an English speaker too, so it was ideal really.

On 5 August there was a site inspection with Chloe, organised by the police. First of all we went to Milan via Bianconi and the warehouse where she was abducted. We went there, Chloe, I and the police, and one of the policeman had a camera. Chloe told everything in front of the tape. In Milan that wasn't so hard, but then we had to go to the small town of Lemie near Turin. She was held captive in Borgial, a tiny place that just consists of a few ruined houses close to Lemie.

At the house where she was held – actually I wouldn't call it a house – at the *place* she was held, Chloe became quite upset. She did spill a couple of tears and I told her everything was going to be OK and that was the last step of her reconstruction. And everyone was very kind with her, the police were very kind. Even though nobody spoke English they had an interpreter, which was sufficient. We spent the whole day in Borgial and Lemie. Chloe managed to describe, very well, every piece of furniture in the house. She managed to recount everything, all the things that happened in that place, for the tape. I was very proud of her. She has great strength and courage.

I haven't dealt with anything like this before. I'm a young lawyer; thirty-one. My mother, she has, but not on this scale in terms of media interest. I have dealt with ISIS, so you get used to seeing bad things. This is the job, to deal with bad things and bad people, otherwise you wouldn't do criminal law. You'd do civil law, mitigation, court law, and that would be even better from a financial point of view, but that isn't the point. Once we went to Borgial, and had the seen the place where she was held... I didn't sleep very well that night, even behind all the barriers you build around yourself as a criminal lawyer, a self-protection, if you like, when you do this particular kind of job. I couldn't help imagining being held in that place. It was very bad; it is indescribable. The conditions...the idea of not seeing your family any more... You don't even know where you are because they drugged you, kidnapped you, drove you. You could have been in France, Germany, Switzerland, Italy, you wouldn't know. There was nobody there, nobody else around, and she was terrified. I felt more than protective. I felt angry.

After seeing her describe the place where she was handcuffed and the bag she was held in, and then seeing it for real... I just felt so angry with those guys. Why would you do something like that? There was no sense to it. Even from a criminal's point of view, it was pointless. There was no gratification, no reason to do this. Especially if you don't have this organisation that you told her you had, and if you don't really plan to sell her. Because that was the point – it was a scam. They tried to make money out of her but then they realised no one was going to pay, as there were so many police forces out – the Italian police, the secret service. Police forces all over Europe were looking for these guys. There were Italians, British, French… Interpol was mediating, and everyone was on the case. All the forces were out. It was a huge thing.

And everyone believed her; that was never in question. The Polish police, Italian police, British police, the DA from three countries – everyone. So when you read in the British tabloids that her story didn't add up – to me, that's strange. Of course, I understand that some bits are not that normal; some bits are strange for a kidnapping. Your kidnapper, take him, for example. This is a guy who took Chloe to the consulate – it is a rescuers' palace! And shopping. I understand that people don't understand that. But the thing is, Chloe can't explain the weirdness either. Why would she? Why do people expect her to understand what went on? She told me she believed that everywhere she went there were people from this criminal group, Black Death, watching her. She thought that playing nice was the best thing to do and that paid off, didn't it? It was the best thing she could do.

★ ★ ★

The issue of many people still not believing her is, I think, the worst part of this case. It's awful for Chloe and I don't understand it. I ask them, if she managed to convince a hundred people from the DA's office – and I believe they are more prepared than a tabloid journalist – why are you still not believing her? Mrs Boccassini – who is a woman who deals with the Mafia every day, and some of the worst criminals ever – they are convinced she's telling the truth. What is wrong with everybody else?

People say Chloe did this for money. And I believe she made a little bit of money from some interviews but not that much. And I'm telling you something: I wouldn't face an ordeal like she has faced for a few thousand pounds. And then you have to find an accomplice. Someone who is willing to risk twenty to twenty-five years in jail for you to make a little bit of money. That is even less credible, isn't it? And yet, that is the conspiracy theory that some people believe.

In Italy, kidnappings were the 'thing' in the '70s, *the* crime. The Sardinians had this business that roughly translates in English to 'anonymous kidnappings'. They dealt with kidnappings of children and entrepreneurs and rich people for years. So we had laws especially written for this, and the police became specifically trained in that area. They were expert in facing those sort of scenarios, in kidnappings. So now, in Italy, no one gets kidnapped any more. It is extremely rare. If you are the parents of the abducted child or missing person all of your bank accounts are frozen straight away by the authorities so you can't pay the ransom. So nobody kidnaps anyone in Italy any more; there is no financial point in doing it if you are a criminal. And this country is the worst place to commit this type of crime. Our investigators are very well trained, so it was a mistake. They made a mistake.

Think like a criminal for a minute. If you wanted to get

$100,000 or a lot of money, yes, it's a bad thing to do it but it still has a purpose. From a criminal point of view, of course, not a normal person's point of view, the result of such a crime is that you end up with the money.

But that was actually not the case here. They didn't think it through. They thought they could get money but they couldn't. And they realised they couldn't. It was just pure torture for the girl. And it's not like she is a thirty-year-old SAS agent who can deal with this sort of thing mentally. We are talking about a twenty-year-old Page 3 model. She's a very nice girl, very intelligent, but she is little more than a girl.

★ ★ ★

There is also an unspoken rule among criminals in Italy. In Italy's prison system, there is an 'honour code'. So if you harm women and children, that is exceptionally bad, a big no-no in our country. Mr Herba, who was in a supermax jail on the outskirts of Milan, on the third or fourth day after Chloe was released, discovered the penalty for such a crime. The inmates have TVs in the cells and his face came up. It flashed up as 'the suspect accused of kidnapping Chloe Ayling'. Ten inmates went into his cell and beat the shit out of him. He was beaten to a pulp. There are people who are serving life in that jail, so it was just fun for them that day to beat the guy who kidnapped a girl. It's like this: you don't hurt women or children. You could be a serial killer and kill a hundred people as long as they are not women and children. I found the papers documenting this in the police files. He was transferred to another jail after that because he couldn't stay there any more. He is now being detained in prison in Pavia, the Casa Circondariale di Pavia.

* * *

Mr Herba's trial began in December [2017]. Chloe didn't need to partake and she didn't want to. The speed of every trial is based on the evidence that the DA office has to bring in front of the judge and, in the case of Mr Herba, they had tons of evidence.

Not simply from what Chloe has said, and all the physical evidence collected from the house, but things he has said himself. He is so foolish. From the prison, on the second day after his arrest, he called his mother. He told her, in Polish, to call a contact and dump the car. He then told her to give him the password for an internet/email account. The password was 'twattwat1'. That isn't a joke. He instructed his mother to do all of this, to destroy the evidence, and for some reason the guy didn't think that phone calls in prison are recorded. Really? Of course the authorities were listening, especially as there was a pending investigation on his case. Everyone was listening to him, and the transcript of that conversation was sent to Scotland Yard.

At the very beginning, when he was first arrested, the police and I thought that Lukasz must be a genius. We were convinced this was a guy who must have a masterplan behind everything. Why would he risk going inside the consulate?

There must be something more he had planned. There must be…we were sure of it. The police and I were questioning his behaviour the whole time. But then it turned out there was nothing. He is clueless.

Kidnapping Chloe and then releasing her at the consulate? I have no idea why he did it. The police have no idea and Chloe certainly didn't. Not that anyone was complaining – it was the best outcome; we didn't need to find her, she was just brought back.

His original plan was to leave her twenty minutes away, which would have been the best thing to do – at least he would be away. Of course, the police would have caught him eventually because of CCTV cameras, but it would have been the best thing for him to do initially. But he didn't. He just walked her inside. Maybe he felt affectionate towards her. I believe the guy had a thing for Chloe but he never expressed it and that is just speculation. But bringing her inside the consulate? It just makes no sense. There are armed soldiers in front of the building; in front of every big consulate in Italy we have the military, for obvious reasons. But even they didn't deter him. Once he had seen those guys, he could have let her go. But he didn't. He decided to walk her inside. So they went inside and she met Nicoletta and straight away told her, 'I'm Chloe Ayling.' Her name was on the missing-people list, on the DEFCON 1 list – the highest alert possible. She was brought into a room straightaway, and of course they didn't just let Mr Herba go or allow him in the room with her. He was immediately arrested. Why did he do this? What we thought at first was that he was either a genius or an idiot. We are tempted now to exclude the first. The police are certainly convinced it's the second.

And the biggest point to the story is that Herba didn't actually deny he kidnapped her either. He never denied it, not even during the hearing. He didn't think that through. I have no idea what will happen at the trial. The crime he is charged with, 'kidnapping in order to extort money', carries a twenty to twenty-five-year sentence. But it could end any way. Professionally, no lawyer ever makes a prediction.

Would he take an insanity plea? He could, I suppose. I had a client once who killed his wife when she was in the shower. He stabbed her thirty-seven times. He started singing while he stabbed her and he went on singing while in hospital and in prison. We managed to get him convicted under partial insanity because he was just that, insane. But an insane man wouldn't be able to come up with such a plan: getting a car, building a fake website, planning to drug a victim... Mr Herba is mad but he's not that kind of insane. He understood what he was doing; the problem was he thought he could get away with it, that he could do it with no problem, like in the movies. That doesn't happen. The trial is in front of the grand jury and he is also facing the toughest DA office. They are the best at fighting the worst kind of crimes. He will be facing his biggest enemies.

My mother told me that during the hearing with Chloe, Lukasz did try to cut a deal with the DA. Lukasz went to Mrs Ferrari and said, 'If you let me go, I will give you all the names of the other people who are involved in this.' The DA started laughing, and said, 'Why don't you stay here because we already know those names.' He just went silent after that. He thought maybe he would be let go, like in an American thriller, but it doesn't happen like that. You will stay in jail and rot in jail until you speak, and when you speak you will still rot in that jail. We're not letting you go. There is no deal for those kinds of people. He needs to stay in jail. It's better for everybody.

So what of this so-called criminal organisation? What of Black Death? If there is, in fact, an organisation called Black Death then we will stop them. But we found a fake website, and on that we found three ads that were for girls, for sale. But we believe that website to be a scam; they offer services they are never going to provide but you are asked to pay half of the money in advance. Then you won't have a clue where your money went. I believe that's the extent of the whole 'Black Death' thing. Just a scam. It was too strange to be true. Interpol and five countries' police forces found nothing.

Not everybody is a stupid cop; we have got very good people working for us. The guys investigating Chloe's case – the guys who didn't sleep for a week to watch all the videos of Herba [and his accomplice] on CCTV cameras – everyone cared and worked hard. We are very passionate, we are Italians, and we do have our problems but we do have some moral conduct rules for criminals and cops alike. We do have respect. So kidnapping a girl to sell her online to the Middle East for sex…that isn't something the Mafia would do. They sell drugs, or commit financial fraud. But not this.

I know Chloe has come to terms with what has happened to her now, but I think the worst part is not being believed.

And who can blame her for feeling hurt when she is mocked and abused by the media or people on Twitter or Instagram? Seeing girls taking pictures of themselves curled up inside bags to mock her and then posting them on social media. Don't get me wrong, I understand 'doubt'. Doubt is great. It is what allows our species to become what we are. Doubting and questioning things is cool, it's a very intelligent thing to do. But doubt must always be balanced or measured in front of reality and in front of evidence. So there is the famous legal term, 'beyond reasonable doubt'. And in my opinion there is evidence beyond reasonable doubt that Mr Herba did kidnap Chloe Ayling. There was no great masterplan. He just messed up.

CHAPTER 18

The Trial of
Lukasz Herba

The trial of Lukasz Herba, who was charged with kidnapping Chloe Ayling, began on 13 December 2017. Mr Herba's lawyer, a Polish attorney working in Milan called Katia Kolakowska, requested that Chloe return to Italy to give evidence in court in person. The judge, Ilio Mannucci Pacini, denied the request, saying that the pre-trial testimony she gave to the Italian police would be used in the court hearing and she would not have to return.

'The fact that she doesn't have to face Herba in court is a huge relief for her,' confirmed Francesco Pesce. 'She really doesn't want to see him again.' The hearing was then adjourned until February 2018.

On 7 February 2018, Mr Herba, dressed all in grey, was led into court in handcuffs as his trial began. It was being held at the Corte di Assise di Milano and was composed of two magistrates and six so-called 'popular' (meaning 'of the people') judges. Their task was to decide all together the verdict of the case, guided by the two judges – or president and vice president of the court, as they are officially known.

Mr Herba was led into a caged section of the courtroom to begin with but, upon the request of his lawyer, he was allowed to sit on a bench next to her.

The trial opened with the prosecuting team, headed by senior investigator, Serena Ferrari, telling the court that the kidnap was a crime of 'enormous gravity'. Police investigators described how: 'Ms Ayling had suffered physical violence, including being drugged, handcuffed and brutally transported inside a suitcase.'

They presented the case to the court that Mr Herba had drugged Chloe with Ketamine and transported her in a canvas bag to a remote farmhouse where she was held for six days. The DA and prosecuting team described how she had been handcuffed and threatened to scare her into being complicit to Mr Herba's demands. They then explained how there were over fifty witnesses involved in the case – police investigators, forensic investigators, scientific experts and technical experts who would be called to present their evidence against Mr Herba.

The jury was told that, before the kidnapping, Herba had been trying to find out how to create the deadly poisons ricin and cyanide at home. Court documents, prepared by police computer experts, showed that he was using eleven different email addresses and had repeatedly searched for the words 'Chloe Ayling', 'Black Death', 'sex-trafficking' and 'ketamine' online. Police forensic analyst Alessandro Granziera said: 'We found searches for a number of sites that explain how to extract pure ricin. He also wrote two emails to one of these sites asking about production, asking for information about what kind of gloves to wear, and how to distil and handle ricin.'

Prosecutors told the court how Mr Herba was also recorded having a telephone conversation with his mother from prison, telling her how to delete the emails.

Images were shown of the large black bag that Herba allegedly used to carry Chloe after he drugged her in Milan and loaded her into his car for the drive to Viu, near Turin. The court was then told that police witnesses had claimed an accomplice was also involved in the kidnapping. A text message from Mr Herba to this accomplice was read out in court: 'Buy a big trip bag. Very big. You know for what [purpose] it serves so you know how big it should be.' CCTV footage was also shown to the jury of the two men together in Milan the day before the alleged kidnapping.

Emails were then read out that had been sent by Mr Herba to Phil Green, Chloe's agent from Supermodel Agency. 'I am MD, a medium-level killer representing Black Death. The girl has been taken and she will be auctioned online in the Middle East.'

Herba sat and shook his head several times as the email was read out. Up until that point he had made no visible sign of disagreement or shown any sort of reaction when evidence was presented or witnesses interviewed. Police investigators told the court that Lukasz Herba posed as a 'mythomaniac adventurer' who claimed to have kidnapped and killed before, in Afghanistan and Iraq, and that he used a false name to initially contact Mr Green for a photo shoot in Paris. It was scheduled for April 2017, and Chloe had flown to France, but Herba cancelled at the last minute, claiming his cameras had been stolen. Police officers told the court they believed this was the start of the kidnap planning.

On 19 February, video footage was shown to the court of Chloe revisiting the farmhouse where she was allegedly held captive. The court heard her say, 'Oh my God,' as she approached the property. Crime scene specialist Gianluca Simontacci is heard telling Chloe that she had to return to help with the investigation. The footage showed Chloe walking up a grassy slope towards the farmhouse before entering the house with officers. She was wearing blue gloves and pointing to parts of the house where she said she was held during her six days.

Francesco Pesce then explained to the jury the significance of the video. 'The videos that were shown by the police were clarifying; she was explaining and describing everything without having any doubt and she was doing this in front of four policemen – this is self-explanatory. She was indoctrinated to believe that [Black Death agents] were around the place and they were willing to kill her if she tried anything. That was not true, of course, but she couldn't know that. She didn't even know where she was. She could have been in France. She had no idea she was in Italy. The city... the town, is not far from the border so, even if she wanted to, there was no way to escape safely — and she is a model, not a policeman or agent; it's normal.'

Photographs were also shown of the Milan studio from where prosecutors claim she was kidnapped. The photos included an advert bearing Chloe's name found on the floor at the studio. Trainers and her discarded clothing were in another photo. The judge and jury were then shown an image of her black carry-on suitcase with her wallet left on top. Mr Herba showed no signs of any emotion or reaction when these photographs were being shown.

The court was later told by a police forensic scientist that traces of the drug Ketamine were found in hair samples taken from Chloe when she was released. They also explained how they found a needle mark on her hand that was not visible to the naked eye. Photographs of Chloe that appeared online and in the photo sent to her agent, Phil Green, showed her with dilated pupils consistent with being drugged.

Mr Herba told the court that day that he did not knowingly take part in any crime, and he described Chloe as 'free, chilled and relaxed' when he met her on 10 July. His lawyer, Katia Kolakowska, declared the kidnap a stunt that Chloe was part of. 'They wanted to create noise around this abduction, they wanted it to go into all the newspapers, and they wanted people to talk about it. Everything was done so that it would become news and for it to be spoken of. I have never seen an abduction that ends like this.'

She told the court that her client would testify at the next hearing and that he would explain that the kidnapping was a ploy to give Ms Ayling's modelling career a boost.

The day ended with a witness giving evidence that he had seen Chloe and Lukasz several times in one day and thought they were boyfriend and girlfriend. Pietro Pellegrino – who lives in Borgial, where Chloe was held – said he saw the pair together in a Volvo and Herba appeared to be holding her hand. He told the court that Herba had always been very kind and said hello when he had seen him in the remote hamlet.

Police then presented CCTV footage of Herba and Chloe walking hand-in-hand together the day before she was released. The video shows them walking next to each other on a street in the hamlet of Viu, near the house where she was allegedly held, the police spokesperson reported.

But while the defence was keen to show this as evidence that Chloe was complicit in her kidnapping, suspicions of a 'publicity stunt' were quickly shut down by Mr Pesce, who had told *The Times*: 'She was terrified after Herba told her that everyone they saw was a member of the group and would kill her if she didn't play nice. There was also an element of grooming mixed with the threats. In the video you can see her holding her other hand across her chest, as if protecting herself. This is not a loving couple. She was probably just trying to keep him calm.'

On 21 February the packed courtroom heard evidence from Herba for the first time. He spoke in Polish when he addressed the court, and through a translator said, 'Chloe collaborated with the kidnapping because once it was finished this would have made her famous and she would have earned a lot of money.'

When asked by prosecutor Mr Paolo Storari if he remembered writing the ransom email to Phil Green, in which he demanded £230,000 and described himself as a medium-level killer with Black Death, Mr Herba stated: 'I remember it well. I wrote it together with the girl.'

He described how they would often leave the house together to pass the time: 'Often we went out because there was nothing to do in the house. We went to buy stuff for her; she didn't even have a toothbrush.'

Herba's translator was appointed by the court. This person was Polish but also spoke fluent Italian. It is worth mentioning this to show that nothing could have been misinterpreted or that Mr Herba could use the excuse that he didn't understand any of the questioning or what was going on.

Mr Pesce then questioned the defendant, as he'd claimed Chloe was a wiling participant in the kidnapping. Speaking softly through the translator, Herba said, 'When Chloe and I met in the studio, I have told her the plan. We have remained talking for almost two hours. I have told her about the plan. She knew that when the scandal finished she would earn lots of money.'

He was then cross-examined by his own lawyer and told the court that he thought Chloe was a 'beautiful woman' but denied having any sexual relationship with her. He said he'd met Chloe over Facebook in 2015, and that this was when the kidnap idea was first hatched, but she backed down because she entered into a relationship. He told the packed courtroom that he contacted her again after seeing on Facebook that the relationship had ended and that he then arranged through her agent for her to go to Paris for a modelling job in April 2017. He said he told her of the kidnapping plot at that point but she refused as she didn't like the venue where she would be staying.

The judge cross-examined Herba at this point, telling the defendant he had made up both the Black Death group, which he claimed was behind the kidnapping, and deep-web auctions of women and a series of Romanian co-conspirators. Mr Herba acknowledged that he built a website where women were advertised to the highest bidder and described himself as a killer-for-hire who had worked for the FBI, CIA and Mossad. He said he only made those claims to draw attention to the site to bring greater notoriety when he would eventually kidnap Ms Ayling. Herba said the Black Death group was solely his invention. He also revealed that his accomplice was convinced throughout that the kidnapping was real. Herba testified that he changed his story because Chloe had backed out of a pledge to cast blame elsewhere in case of his arrest. He also denied his initial statements to investigators after his arrest that he needed to earn money to treat his leukaemia, saying he wasn't ill.

It was at this point that prosecutor Paolo Storari asked the court for a psychiatric evaluation of the defendant, citing the many contradictions in his story. The DA was speechless. It was unheard of for a defendant to change their story during the trial process and the defence team was shocked. Proceedings suddenly stopped.

'So everything you told us before was a lie? You have lied and now you are telling us another story?' was the line of questioning from Mr Pesce. The DA and defence team couldn't believe that Mr Herba had suddenly decided to change everything he had previously told the police.

'They actually thought they were on a candid-camera type show,' Mr Pesce confirmed later. 'It was so surreal, everyone was shocked. It was just a big joke. The judge overruled the decision. No psychiatric evaluation was needed because here was a man who had claimed to be all these things and was now just changing his story because he thought it would help his case. The judge decided that Mr Herba was very capable of thinking and acting on his own thoughts and he understood what he was doing. It wasn't going to work.'

★ ★ ★

On 20 March, a defence medical witness, Dr Domenico Di Candia, said he had carried out drug tests on Chloe's urine and hair in July 2017. In a report filed to the court he said that the urine sample was negative but the 2cm hair strand showed traces of ketamine. Dr Di Candia explained to the court: 'Given that hair grows at about 1cm a month, the 2cm sample showed that ketamine had been periodically consumed two months before the event.' Evidence of Chloe's DNA being inside the holdall bag used to take her to the remote farmhouse was also disputed by Mr Herba, who told the court that she had got in herself to leave her DNA.

'I'm telling the truth. It was a plan to help Chloe get publicity. The idea was to make up the kidnap to make her famous.'

The court was adjourned until May 2018, then again until June when the verdict was due to be delivered.

★ ★ ★

On 11 June, at approximately midday, Lukasz Herba was found guilty of kidnapping and extortion and sentenced to sixteen years and nine months in jail.

On this announcement, Chloe made this statement: 'Lukasz is guilty. It is official now. Now the world knows what I have known all along: he is guilty. Perhaps all those people who thought they knew all about the case just by reading unreliable news reports or making assumptions about me will think twice before making such judgements again.

Thank you to all who believed in me from the beginning. Justice has been served by punishing the kidnapper with a nearly seventeen-year jail sentence for what he has done to me and I am so very happy this is all over. I can now get closure on what has been a terrible time. I am desperate to put the ordeal behind me and move on with my life. I want to forge a new path now that the world can see I was telling the truth.

It's time to move on.'

CHAPTER 19

Reflections

I am adding this section as I believe it's important to show the reasoning behind certain events in the book. At the time, I just believed what I was told and reacted accordingly, but certain situations have since been explained to me, and the Italian police have helped piece things together. And so this section will have references to what I was told after the event. I can only react to things that happened to me at the time, but now I have the benefit of hindsight and the police investigation too, and I think it's important to include it all so you get the whole picture.

For example: I was told that the terrorist attack the night I was in Paris had spooked Lukasz, as the police presence around the capital increased dramatically. The plan was to kidnap me that morning in Paris but it was too risky with the police and authorities on high alert. They aborted that plan and told me a fake story about a robbery to cancel the shoot. What does that feel like? To look back and think, I had a lucky escape that time. That a terrorist attack on the city had, in fact, helped save me. That that was the first attempt someone made to kidnap me. I wouldn't be so lucky the next time.

Now I know why that photo shoot had been cancelled, and it wasn't anything to do with a burglary. The tale that 'Andre' told me about a burglary was a lie. The line he kept telling me, that 'At least the motorbike was still there', was simply a lie to reassure me that the whole situation sounded believable.

The level of detail in the Milan photo shoot email... that is what gets me now. How much effort had gone into making everything seem normal and genuine? And the detail about the studio being on the street where he lived. I had no questions, no concerns, no worries in the slightest. You don't need to be in the industry to see that he took a lot of time and effort to make it convincing, make it authentic. Even down to the lie that he had asked an air-conditioning engineer to make sure the air con was working properly for me when I arrived.

I constantly think back to the day I arrived at that studio for what I thought would be the photo shoot. I wish I could have messed up their plans somehow. What if I had said to the man calling himself 'Daniel', when I first spoke to him, 'No, I'm not coming in; you come outside and meet me.' What would have happened then? Would they have come out to meet me? Would one of them taken off their mask and pretended to be a photographer? I don't know.

Or what if I had arrived with a boyfriend? Or a couple of girlfriends? What would have happened then? Would they have taken all of us? They had only planned one syringe, so maybe they would have knocked anyone else unconscious or something... I don't know. But these thoughts go through my mind often. I can't help it. It's a huge 'what if' situation. What if, right at the start of this nightmare, I had messed up their plans? But I can't keep thinking like that. They must have been prepared for every situation. They had gone to so much effort already that perhaps no matter what I'd done they would still have got me.

The police believe that the masked man who never spoke for the first few hours I was at the house was, in fact, Lukasz. I couldn't tell you if it was or not, but I suppose that makes sense of the fact that the masked man didn't speak – otherwise I might have recognised his voice. And there were only three sets of DNA found at the house, too. Mine, Lukasz's and that of another male. Lukasz claimed the masked man was Romanian; unmasked man was the driver, and then there was him and me.

Lukasz told me his mum had been kidnapped but I have since been told that his mum lives in Poland. He told me another story about how he didn't know who his parents were and that 'CK' was going to help him track them down. He also told me he was going out to burn the ID card with 'Daniel' on it but the police found it on him when they arrested him. Why he went through the charade of going outside, telling me he was going to burn it and destroy it, I don't know. He was gone for a good ten to fifteen minutes.

The police found traces of semen on the bed where Lukasz had masturbated.

Lukasz took me to the consulate and not the police station because he believed they would fly me back to the UK straightaway. He thought that they would investigate my kidnapping in England and then I would be able to tell the police I didn't want that to happen.

The police officers in the original interview, Gianluca and Serena, were brilliant. They were so understanding and sympathetic. Gianluca was always the one to help me if I needed information. I didn't see Serena much after the initial interview, but Gianluca would always be around and would see me if I needed him. He would always visit me with a different police officer but he would never send police officers without him. Unless I saw Gianluca, I wouldn't feel totally safe. Unless it was him and someone else, I wasn't happy. He knew that and made sure he was always there to reassure me.

The third kidnapper with the beard, who I believed to be in the car at first, has always bugged me. Until recently. I was looking through the newspapers when I saw the CCTV pictures that had been released. He was pictured walking down the street in Milan twenty-four hours before I was kidnapped. It was Lukasz but with a beard. It was either fake or he later shaved it off. Either way I knew it was him in the car; it was him with the beard.

So, what have I learnt from this? Firstly that I have experienced something most people won't ever have to deal with. I did everything in a way that I felt was right. There is no concrete or set way of acting in certain situations. Everyone reacts differently to things. Secondly, I know there are people you can trust and people you can't trust. Never meet people in real-life that you have met online. I have learnt there are only certain things in life that matter and only certain people in life that matter.

And lastly, a thank you. I am so lucky to have been surrounded by people that cared for me after what happened. The police, Filippo, Carlo, Francesco, Nicoletta, Kruger Cowne... having these people around have helped in my recovery and I am very grateful to them.

Epilogue

I went out walking Nylah the other day. It was a crisp, fresh morning and her excitement when I put her on her lead and led her out of the door was very satisfying. I love doing that sort of thing again. I had taken it for granted before but now I'm able to enjoy the simplicity of a good couple of hours spent walking my dog and wearing her out.

But halfway into our walk we heard a gunshot and that was it. As soon as she hears a bang or a firework, she's gone, scared stiff. I cursed myself for not keeping her on the lead. I knew I should have, but she loves being free and running around, and it never seems fair to restrain her. I couldn't find her anywhere. I was calling and calling and calling her. I kept on walking, thinking I would catch up with her or would see her somewhere, hiding in the bushes, but she could have gone anywhere; she has the flight instinct when she is scared.

I was waiting and watching and calling her for what

seemed like ages. In the end I rang my mum. She was so upset. I knew she would be. She started working herself up and crying that Nylah wouldn't ever come back, that she was gone for ever. 'First you, then the dog… another one to go missing!' she said, crying.

I think in a way that sums up what has happened. I went missing but I survived. I came back. I came back to a torrent of interest, of fascination and then of speculation, of people talking about me who don't know the real me or the real story. I am hoping you can now understand what has happened and that everything I did, how I acted, how I behaved, was because I didn't want to die. I can't change who I am. Do I want to sue everyone who has belittled me, called me a liar, abused me and sent hateful messages? No, I just want to carry on with my life. And speaking of which, I have a little boy to cuddle and a dog to walk. Nylah came back too – eventually. She was handed in to the vet. I went to get her and she was tired and muddy but so pleased to see me that her tail would not stop wagging. She was pleased to be going home.

I know how that feels.